IMPORTANT NOTICE

Do not use this book until you have read these pages.

You have in your hands one half of the system that will change your life. To achieve success it is essential that you download the other half of this system from the Hay House website:

hayhouse.com/mckenna

and use the audio sessions that complete it.

This is not just a book to read, it is part of a life-changing solution. This book is the first essential element of the system. The audio sessions are just as important: you must use both the book and the audio sessions to achieve permanent success.

The sessions contain everything I would do if I were working with you personally. They include simple, powerful psychological techniques and a hypnotic trance that strengthen the power of your subconscious mind to guide your success.

The sessions are really easy to download onto your computer or smartphone, just a few clicks, then a few minutes later, you will have me there whenever you need, to help you make the changes you want.

Intellectual knowledge is not the same as real change, so you cannot expect lasting results if you only read this book. You must download and use the psychological techniques and guided hypnosis to achieve permanent, positive change.

In hypnotic trance your unconscious is highly receptive to positive intentions. It is not the same as sleep, it is a wonderful state of deep relaxation, like a daydream or meditation, and even though you are deeply relaxed, if for any reason you need to awaken, you will do so with all the resources you need.

The audio techniques are not just essential, they are also enjoyable and rewarding. In fact, many people use them over and over to reinforce their new mind-set and enhance their success.

Ensure your success now. Go online now to:

hayhouse.com/mckenna

1. Input the product ID and download code shown below (also found on the card at the front of this book) and then download the free sessions right now:

Product ID: 3016

Download code: mckenna

2. Regularly use the sessions as directed in this book.
3. Enjoy it and relax, knowing you are now on your way to lasting success!

SUPERCHARGE YOUR INTELLIGENCE TODAY!

PAUL MCKENNA, PH.D.

EDITED BY MICHAEL NEILL

HAY HOUSE, INC.
Carlsbad, California • New York City
London • Sydney • Johannesburg
Vancouver • New Delhi

Published and distributed in the United States by: Hay House, Inc.:
www.hayhouse.com® • **Published and distributed in Australia by:**
Hay House Australia Pty. Ltd.: www.hayhouse.com.au • **Published and
distributed in the United Kingdom by:** Hay House UK, Ltd.: www.hay
house.co.uk • **Published and distributed in the Republic of South Africa by:** Hay House SA (Pty), Ltd.: www.hayhouse.co.za • **Distributed in
Canada by:** Raincoast Books: www.raincoast.com • **Published in India
by:** Hay House Publishers India: www.hayhouse.co.in

Cover design: Alex Tuppen • *Interior photos/illustrations:*

Previously published in Great Britain in 2012 by Bantam Press, an imprint of Transworld Publishers, ISBN: 9780593064054.

Cataloging-in-Publication Data is on file at the Library of Congress

Tradepaper ISBN: 978-1-4019-4897-9

10 9 8 7 6 5 4 3 2 1
1st edition, March 2017

Printed in the United States of America

HOW TO USE THE HYPNOTIC TRANCE DOWNLOADS IN THIS BOOK

This is more than a book—it's a system designed to boost your brainpower. It comes with two powerful hypnotic trances that will fill your unconscious mind with positive thoughts and feelings and support you in becoming smarter. You can find the details on the special card at the front of the book.

1. Smarter While You Sleep

Repeated listening to this track while you go to bed at night will help you glide into a wonderful deep night sleep while helping your creativity to evolve your mind so that you access more of your full potential and become sharper and smarter.

2. Exam Confidence

This trance is designed to be used in the buildup to any sort of exam or situation where you need to be at your best. Regular listening will massively reduce any fear and reduce the pressure associated with taking exams. It will also help make you feel calm and in control on the day of the exam so you can easily access all the information you need from your amazing mind.

While the hypnotic trances will have a powerful impact in and of themselves, they are designed to activate certain suggestions and strategies I have installed throughout the book. For maximum effect, you *must* use the hypnotic trances in conjunction with the book.

**Do not use the hypnotic trances while driving
or operating machinery.**

• • •

A BRIEF WORD
FROM PAUL MCKENNA

You are about to become smarter!

By the time you have finished this book, practiced the techniques, and listened to the hypnotic trances, you will be using far more of your mind's potential than you are right now. You will find learning easier, more relaxed, and more enjoyable than you've ever dreamed possible before. And when you are called on to put your knowledge to the test, you will do so with greater confidence and greater success than ever before.

But this book isn't just about becoming better at passing exams. It's about doing better in every area of your life!

Scientists have now discovered that the limitations on human potential are not down to genetics—they're down to our ability to unlock the full, rich capacity of our mind and brain. As you become smarter, you will surprise yourself with what you are able to learn and understand. You will notice that you are able to adapt more quickly to a wide variety of situations. You will demonstrate greater flexibility in your thinking and therefore gain greater control over your environment and over your world.

On a practical level, you will begin to read faster and your memory will improve. Your concentration will increase and your creativity will go through the roof. Best of all, you'll begin making smarter decisions because you'll be seeing the world with greater clarity. This will improve the quality of results you create in the world, and you'll feel better about yourself and your life as a result.

Over the course of this book, I'm going to demonstrate to you time and time again that you are already smarter than you think—and that this is only the beginning. The individual elements of this system have been tested over many years and with tens of thousands of people. They are based on cutting-edge scientific research into the brain and include all of the best techniques and principles that I have found through many years of research into increasing intelligence, creativity, and effectiveness.

Quite simply, if you want to become smarter, all you need to do is follow my instructions, practice the techniques, and listen to the hypnotic trances regularly. I will take care of all the rest.

In order to help you along the way, you will notice some slightly unusual features to the way this book is structured:

1. "Get into the Zone" Warm-Ups

As you progress through the book, you will find a series of "Get into the Zone" warm-ups that will expand and change as you learn more. If you're feeling a bit stuck, these simple techniques will get you into an optimal state for learning the material in each chapter, allowing you to get more out of yourself and more from what you find inside.

2. Smarter Techniques

Throughout each chapter, you will find techniques to make you smarter. You may find some of these exercises simple, while others may seem a bit more challenging at first. While you do not have to do every technique in order, it is important to practice each one a minimum of three times in order to ensure that you begin to notice its effects. Many of the techniques are designed to be reinforced by suggestions and processes in the hypnotic trances.

3. Calls to Action

These practical "real world applications" are designed to both illustrate and practice ideas discussed in the text. While you don't have to stop and complete each call to action before reading on, putting them into practice will bring multiple rewards over time.

4. Chapter Summaries and Mind Maps

At the end of each chapter, you will find a bullet-pointed summary of all the key ideas in that chapter on one page. You will also find a visual summary called a "mind map." Even though these mind maps may look simple, this extraordinary whole brain learning technology gives your brain another way to access and process the information from the chapter. You can use these summaries as a way of reviewing the material after reading it, or as a way of priming your unconscious mind by going through them before beginning to read it. Either way, using the summaries and mind maps will make it easier for you to retain and access key information afterwards.

And that's it!

Wherever you're at right now—whether you already consider yourself to be ahead of the game or you feel like you're falling behind—all you need to do is read, relax, enjoy, practice the techniques, and repeatedly listen to the hypnotic trances.

You're smarter than you think, and together we're going to ensure that you get smarter and smarter for life!

To your success,
Paul McKenna

• • •

SUPERCHARGE YOUR INTELLIGENCE TODAY!

EVERYTHING YOU NEED TO KNOW TO GET SMARTER ON ONE PAGE

- You will become smarter the moment you learn to access more of your mind.

- Life is a skill—anything can be learned.

- There are only three things you need to learn anything—access to a resourceful state, implementation of an effective strategy, and time to practice until you have developed the kind of distinctions that lead to mastery.

- We all have multiple intelligences, and every intelligence can be developed.

- Whole brain learning is the key to long-term success—Conscious/Unconscious; Left brain/Right brain; Mind/Body.

- 80 percent of the information you need can be grasped in 20 percent of the time.

- Everything you have ever read or heard is stored as a multisensory recording in the unconscious mind.

- Creativity is a natural function of the mind.

- The solution to any problem is already inside you.

- The future is bigger than you can imagine and yours to create through the decisions you make.

- You can stay sharp at any age by following the golden rule of neuroplasticity—use it or lose it!

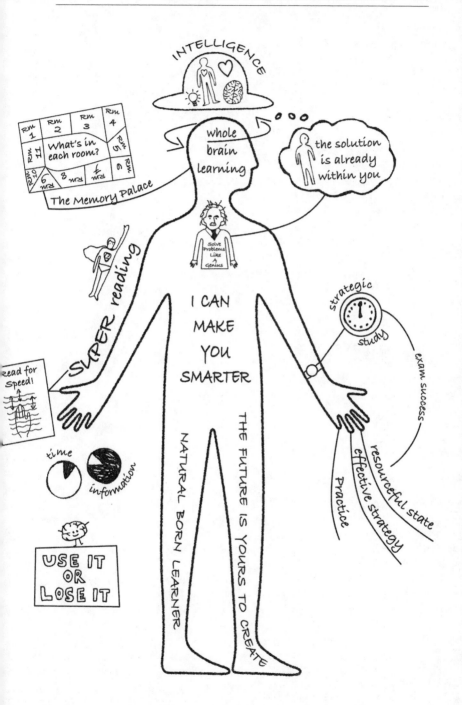

SECTION I

•

YOU'RE SMARTER THAN YOU THINK

In the first section of this book, I am going to be introducing you to the amazing natural capacity of your mind and brain.

As we proceed, you will begin to see yourself as smarter and be able to crank up your concentration, curiosity, and persistence, whenever you want. You will learn to recognize your natural learning abilities and how to tap into your optimal learning states.

As well as clearing out any blocks to learning that you may have picked up along the way, you'll also be able to reprogram your mind for success by moving beyond the limitations of the past and discovering your greater potential. By looking deeper into the origins of "intelligence testing" and cutting-edge scientific research into genius and mastery, you'll discover that it's not so much what you're born with—it's what you do with it.

To learn how easy it can be, let's get started . . .

CHAPTER 1

•

Unlock the Power of Your Mind and Brain

The Power of Hypnosis

One of the first people I ever hypnotized was the son of my next-door neighbor. He came over and knocked on my door and said he had a biology exam the next morning and wondered if hypnosis might help him. Now, George was not a model student, but I was up for the challenge so I invited him in.

I knew that everything that has ever happened in your life is stored as a multisensory recording in the unconscious mind. Your unconscious is that part of you that keeps your heart beating and your body breathing without you having to pay it any attention at all. It's the larger mind—the mind that's in charge of our wisdom, creativity, and deeper intelligence.

The reason we remember some things and forget others isn't that we don't retain the information—it's that most of us have limited ways to access the specific information we want when we want it, even though it's already safely stored in our minds.

So I said to George, "Have you been in class?"

He said, "Oh, yeah, I've been there, but I was a bit bored by it. I wasn't really paying attention."

I said, "No problem. Close your eyes and relax."

While I didn't know then everything I now know about accelerated learning and the power of the mind, I was well versed in the power of a simple, direct suggestion.

I said to him, "Listen carefully. When you're in the exam tomorrow, you'll be able to remember everything that you need to in order to pass your exam, in order to achieve to your fullest potential."

Then I asked him to imagine feeling relaxed in the exam and everything going okay. I had him imagine some challenges arising but handling them well. When we were finished, I woke him up and sent him on his way.

The next day, he came over and knocked on the door. When I opened it he said, "What did you do to me?"

I was a bit concerned, so I invited him in. As soon as he came through the front door he said, "It was amazing! As soon as I sat down all the answers just flowed. I knew the answer to everything. I finished ahead of time. It was just superb."

I was worried that he might have just written a load of rubbish, but he seemed surprisingly confident. He told me he would get his results in a few weeks, so there was nothing left to do but wait.

When his results came through a few weeks later he had done poorly at pretty much everything. He got a D or F in every subject—except biology. In the one subject he had been hypnotized to believe he would succeed in, he got an A.

His teacher thought he'd cheated, but of course he hadn't. He'd tapped into the power of his unconscious mind—something that is available to all of us but seldom used or even talked about. By using his mind in this way, he'd given himself the edge. And in doing that he'd discovered that he was smarter than either of us had thought possible.

The Mind and the Brain

In the West, we generally talk about the mind as though it were divided into two parts: the conscious mind and the unconscious or subconscious mind. The conscious mind is the mind we actively think with all day long. It's the running commentary that's probably going on in your head right now, and it can only concentrate on a small handful of ideas at any one time.

The unconscious mind, on the other hand, is the larger mind. It's the sum total of all our thoughts, our wisdom, creativity, and memories; it's made up of all those parts of ourselves that we are unaware of at any given time. It processes millions of pieces of information every single moment, and is the most powerful biocomputer on the planet.

In the same way, scientists have discovered that the human brain is divided into two hemispheres—the **left brain**, which deals predominantly with logic, linear, and sequential thinking; and the **right brain**, which deals with associations, abstract ideas, creativity, symbolism, and emotions.

Now, predominantly, we are a left brain–dominated culture—in other words, we put a big emphasis upon logic, upon sequence, and upon our ability to speak intelligently about things. For example, when we speak, we don't speak in just random words and ideas, unless we're insane, but generally we have a flow and a sequence to the ideas we express. A story is told in a logical, sequential way. Plenty of people do jobs that require use of their left brain, such as an accountant or a computer programmer. Some people do jobs that involve them thinking in abstract and symbolic ways, such as artists and musicians.

While we may personally value the attributes of one hemisphere over another, in order to operate functionally as a human being, we need to make use of both. In fact, many scientists now believe that true intelligence is not a measure of left or right brain dominance but of the degree of interplay between the two hemispheres. Which is a fancy way of saying that if you want to become smarter, the key is not simply to get better at math, to collect more information, or even to become more creative. It is to learn to use the whole of your mind and the whole of your brain more and more of the time.

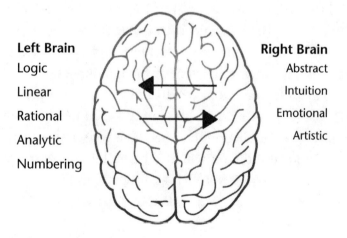

Left Brain
Logic
Linear
Rational
Analytic
Numbering

Right Brain
Abstract
Intuition
Emotional
Artistic

Over the course of this book, I will be giving you a number of techniques designed to bring more balance to your mind and brain. The first is one of the simplest, but also one of the most important.

Originally developed by Dr. Win Wenger, one of the world's foremost researchers and innovators in the fields of intelligence and creative problem-solving, this one exercise, regularly practiced, has been shown to permanently increase measurable intelligence by as much as 40 points. Best of all, it's simple to do, and will get easier and easier every time you do it.

It works by tapping into two of your mind's natural and often undervalued abilities—description and daydreaming. Description is a primarily conscious, left brain activity—it imposes structure and order on our experience by sequencing things in a way that can be written or spoken aloud. Daydreaming, on the other hand, is a primarily unconscious, right brain activity—we allow our minds to wander along through a series of seemingly random images and mental movies.

By describing your daydreams out loud—a process Dr. Wenger calls "image streaming"—you will not only make new connections between your conscious and unconscious mind; you will also be building new neural pathways between your left and right brain.

Here is all you need to do to get started . . .

IMAGE STREAMING

Read the technique all the way through before you start.

1. Close your eyes and become aware of the stream of seemingly random images that are running through your brain.

2. Begin describing aloud what you are seeing, no matter how vague it may be. The simple guideline is to **say what you see! For example:** *I see black, but now a beach begins to appear. I can feel the warmth of the sand between my toes and see the black water lapping against the shore. There's a boat with a man with a handlebar moustache—now the cover of the Beatles' Sgt. Pepper album appears and I can begin to hear the opening music from the album.*

3. If at any point you are having difficulty "seeing" images in your mind's eye, simply describe the darkness. Within five minutes, you will begin to notice patterns emerging and specific images beginning to appear.

It's important that you actually speak what you see out loud. If you just try to follow the image stream without talking, chances are that you will either get lost in your daydream or even fall asleep. By engaging your body as well as your mind in this exercise, you will ensure that you get the most out of everything you have.

In the next chapter, I will show you how to tap into your optimal learning state and unleash the natural learner already inside you . . .

Until then, enjoy this quick review that you'll find at the end of each chapter. On one side of the page, you'll be able to review the key points from the chapter. On the other, you'll see a visual representation of the information in this chapter, known as a "mind map." By combining information in these two formats, your brain will process the information more deeply and it will be easier to retain, recall, and utilize. (You'll also learn how to make mind maps for yourself in Chapter 6!)

THE WHOLE CHAPTER IN ONE PAGE

- **Your mind processes millions of pieces of information every single moment, and is the most powerful biocomputer on the planet.**

- **Everything you have ever read or even heard is stored as a multisensory recording in the unconscious mind.**

- **If you want to become smarter, you need to bring more balance between the two parts of your mind and the two sides of your brain.**

- **Image streaming is a simple exercise that will increase your capacity for learning, problem-solving, creativity, and even your IQ score!**

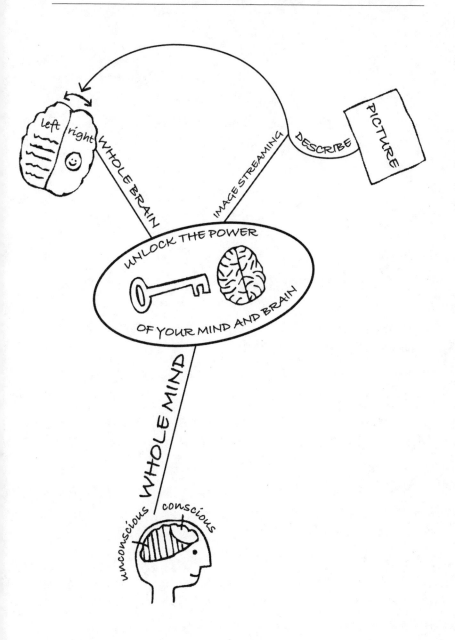

CHAPTER 2

•

You Can
Learn Anything

A Smarter Approach to Learning

In all my research over the years into the possibilities of the human mind, there are only three things I have come across that stop people from learning whatever it is they want to learn:

1. **They are in an unresourceful state of mind.**

2. **They are using an ineffective strategy.**

3. **They do not practice consistently enough to master what they are trying to learn.**

As we progress through this book, you will learn to easily go into resourceful states and to have the most powerful of those states available at your fingertips. I'll give you a number of effective strategies for learning all sorts of different things, and even some simple ways to choose which strategy to employ when. We will also discuss the most effective ways to practice and build powerful states of motivation to continue practicing until the job is done.

Have you ever seen a baby when it's just beginning to learn to walk? It falls over and get back up again and again until it figures it out. Now, imagine that same baby thought like your average adult. The baby would take its first tentative step, fall over, then think back on all the other things it had tried and failed at throughout its life. After a few more halfhearted attempts, it would give up, deciding that this whole walking thing is too hard and too dangerous and something ought to be done about it.

Intuitively, we already know that learning involves practice and in particular trial and error. We don't give up on a baby when it falls over—we don't say, "Oh well, I guess that one's not a walker." We encourage the baby to get back up and try again and again until it can toddle and then walk and run with the best of them.

The fact is you were born able to learn. You've been learning from the moment you were born, and you didn't even have to think about it. You're hardwired for learning. You are a learning machine.

There was a time when you were little and you couldn't speak the way you speak now—but you learned. There was a time you couldn't eat with a knife and fork, but quite naturally you learned how. You couldn't help learning these things, because human beings are natural learners.

No one taught you how to think, but here you are, thinking, and it's amazing—an everyday miracle. After all, you are reading and understanding the words on this page, aren't you?

How did that happen?

How did you learn English well enough to make sense of what I wrote?

Were you born speaking English?

Or were you born with a natural ability to learn?

The point is this:

You are a natural-born learner.

Mind-Sets for Failure and Success

Scientists and researchers have done a number of experiments that demonstrate that your mind-set—that is, your attitude and approach towards learning—is one of the critical factors in how long you stick with something and how well you learn it.

In one of the most startling of the experiments, children who received identical grades on an exam were divided into two groups. The first group was praised for their intelligence, along the lines of "wow—eight out of ten—you're so smart!" The second group was praised for their application, along the lines of "wow—eight out of ten—you must have really worked hard!"

To the researchers' amazement, the children who were told they had done so well because they were smart, what is known as a "fixed mind-set," actually became reluctant to take on further, more advanced tests and even lied about their scores when asked to tell others how they had done. In stark contrast, the children who believed their high scores were the result of their own efforts, known as a "growth mind-set," were eager to take on the more advanced work, and told the truth about their results.

So, what can we learn from this?

The first thing we can see is that mind-set may be even more important than innate ability in determining our results.

The second is that we should become more aware of any areas in school or in life where we may have gotten ourselves stuck in a fixed mind-set. This will often re-veal itself in statements like:

- "I'm just no good at math."
- "I couldn't draw a picture if my life depended on it."
- "I'll never be smart like them."
- "Nobody likes a know-it-all."

Unfortunately, as we grew up, our well-meaning parents, friends, and teachers filled us with ideas like these that had the effect of a hypnotic suggestion. Hypnotic suggestions go directly into the unconscious mind and are quickly accepted as fact without going through a conscious filtering process.

This is why at some point most of us stopped approaching life as learners. We decided instead that we were good at some things and bad at some things and just plain mediocre at most. The problem is that the moment we decide we're not good at something—that we're bad or stupid or even just that we're not smart enough to learn *that*—we shut down our natural, human capacity to learn.

If you've decided that you're a bad student, or that you have a poor memory, or that you're bad at math or not creative or a poor public speaker, chances are you won't take any action to correct the problem. That lack of action makes it unlikely that the situation will change, and you prove yourself right, over and over and over again. It's known as a self-fulfilling prophecy, and it's the exact opposite of learning.

So let's do a simple technique that will begin to reverse the hypnotic suggestions and limiting decisions that get you to stop before you've even started. Each time you do this exercise, you will find it easier to see yourself as smarter and more capable of learning whatever it is you want to learn. As with all the techniques in the book, it's best to read it through in its entirety and then go back and follow my instructions, step-by-step.

SEE YOURSELF SMARTER

Read the technique all the way through before you start.

1. Take three slow and gentle breaths. Allow your body to relax and feel good.

2. Now, imagine what you would look like if you were just a little bit smarter than you are right now. How would you sit? What kind of expression would you have on your face? How would that smarter you show up in the world? How would they smile and interact with other people?

3. Step into that smarter you so that you're seeing what they see, hearing what they hear, and feeling the way they feel.

4. Next, imagine an even smarter you in front of you. How do they sit? What kind of expression do they have on their face? How does that even smarter you show up in the world? How do they smile and interact with other people?

5. Once again step into that smarter you until you see what they see, hear what they hear, and feel the way they feel.

   Repeat as many times as you like, allowing yourself to imagine a smarter and smarter you each time . . .

The Difference That Makes the Difference

All human behavior is the product of our neuro-physiological states—that is, the sum total of every-thing that is going on with us at any one time. What state we are in is down to a combination of how we are physically, how we are emotionally, and how we are psychologically at any given moment.

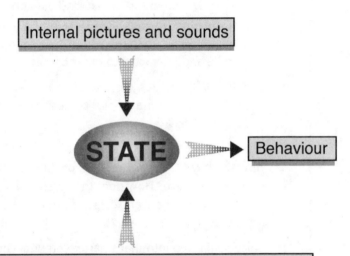

While we all like to feel good, the particular states of mind most prized in the real world are those that not only feel good but also optimize levels of performance. Athletes, for example, call their peak performance state "the zone." They'll often refer to "being in the zone," or even "chasing the zone." In fact, one of the most cited reasons for athletes continuing to compete even after they've reached the top of their field is because they just cherish being in the zone.

Musicians often refer to their optimal performance state as being "in the groove." Even the richest rock stars in the world continue to tour and make albums because they simply love the feeling of being in the groove.

In psychology, we call this optimal state "flow." When you are in the flow of things, you naturally make "all the right moves." You're fully engaged in the whole process, you move in the right way, you're involved in the whole process, it's not too difficult but it's not too easy either.

And the same is true for people who love to learn. It's not so much that they need to have new information or master new skills, but rather that they love the feeling of being in "the learning zone." What this feels like may be slightly different for different people, but for most people the key elements of their natural learning state are remarkably similar. And because there have been times in the past when you've been in an optimal state for learning, you can reaccess that state and harness it any time you choose.

Because the human nervous system cannot tell the difference between a real and a vividly imagined experience, when you remember times where you've been totally absorbed in something you are learning, if you remember them vividly enough, you will begin to reenter that state. Your unconscious will begin to re-create the posture and breathing patterns of that state, your body chemistry will begin to change, and you will notice that the feelings and associations you have with that highly positive state will begin coming easily to mind.

Now, if each time we return to that state we create an associational link to it by squeezing our thumb and finger together, we quickly create a new association between our natural learning state and the squeeze of our thumb and our finger. After a surprisingly short amount of time, the associational link will be made to the point that we can reverse the process. Any time you want to reenter your natural learning state, you will be able to squeeze your thumb and finger together and find yourself effortlessly returning to those feelings.

This is like the famous experiment done in the 1930s by the Russian scientist Ivan Pavlov. Every time he fed his dogs, he rang a bell to create a new neuroassociation. He would feed his dogs, ring the bell, feed the dogs, ring the bell, feed the dogs, ring the bell, until eventually, all he had to do was just ring the bell and the dogs' mouths would begin to salivate. This type of conditioned association is more commonly known as an "anchor."

So . . . how would you like to be able to go into a peak learning state any time you choose?

During this next technique, I'm going to ask you to remember times when you were in your natural learning state—the state of absorbed fascination you approached life with as a child. We're going to return to it like you're back there again now. At the height of the positive feelings, you will squeeze the thumb and middle finger of your right hand together and a new association will be created, "anchoring" the feelings of absorbed fascination to the squeeze of your fingers. This will enable you to quickly and easily enter this state whenever it is appropriate to do so.

REDISCOVERING YOUR NATURAL LEARNING STATE

Read the technique all the way through before you start.

1. Think of something that you find genuinely fasci-
    nating. It might be music, art, swimming, motor-
    cycles, or anything that grabs your attention and
    captures your imagination.

2. When you have chosen something, think of a time
    when you were engrossed in learning about it.
    Return to that time in your imagination now, see-
    ing what you saw, hearing what you heard, and
    feeling how good you felt.

3. Now, as you continue to enjoy exploring this
    memory, make the colors rich and bright and
    bold, make the sounds loud and clear, and the
    feelings strong. Do this until you have really
    amped up the feelings of fascination, absorption,
    and enjoyment.

4. At the height of these feelings, squeeze your
    thumb and middle finger together on your right
    hand to create an associational link between the
    two. Continue to go through the memory in your
    mind as you do so.

5. When you're ready, squeeze the thumb and
    middle finger of your right hand together. Can
    you feel that feeling of absorbed fascination begin-
    ning to come back into your mind and body? If so,
    know that each time you repeat this exercise you
    will strengthen this anchor.

6. If not, simply take a longer break to clear your
    mind and return to this exercise whenever you
    are ready.

Throughout the first section of the book, I will guide you through a series of techniques like this that will enable you to access the kinds of states that lead to learning success and allow you to access more of your mind and brain. You'll learn to crank up your curiosity, concentrate more effectively, and tap into your natural motivation to learn.

For now, take a few moments to review the key ideas from this chapter before moving on to the next . . .

THE WHOLE CHAPTER IN ONE PAGE

- You are a natural-born learner.

- We have all been programmed to believe certain things about how smart we are, how smart it is good to be, and what we are and aren't capable of learning. These unconscious programs are like hypnotic suggestions, limiting our behavior until they become self-fulfilling prophecies.

- There are only three reasons people fail to learn new things—they are in an unproductive state of mind, they are using an ineffective strategy, or they give up too soon.

- All human behavior is the product of our neurophysiological states—that is, the sum total of everything that is going on with us at any one time. What state we are in at any given moment comes down to a combination of how we are physically, how we are emotionally, and how we are psychologically.

- The human nervous system cannot tell the difference between a real and a vividly imagined experience.

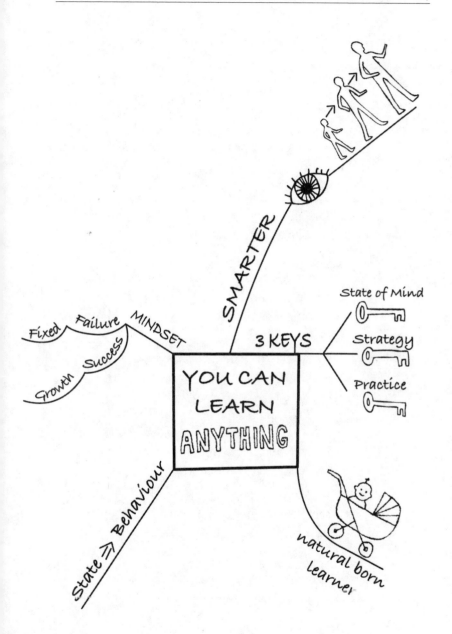

GET INTO THE ZONE!

Before you begin to read this chapter, check in to see if you are in your learning zone. If not, follow the steps below:

1. Take three slow and gentle breaths. Allow your body to relax and feel good.

2. Squeeze your thumb and middle finger together, firing off your "natural learning" anchor until you can begin to feel yourself going into a relaxed state of absorbed fascination.

3. Now, imagine what you would look like if you were just a little bit smarter than you are right now. How would you sit? What kind of expression would you have on your face? How would that smarter you show up in the world? How would they smile and interact with other people?

4. Step into that smarter you so that you're seeing what they see, hearing what they hear, and feeling the way they feel.

When you are ready, begin . . .

CHAPTER 3

•

What's School Got to Do with Getting Smarter?

The Power of Suggestion

When I was growing up, I had one particular teacher who would always shake his head, make a tutting noise, and say to me, "You'll never learn." Since then, I've found that many people have been carrying around not only the idea that they'll never learn, but a whole set of reasons for why they think that might be true.

Unless you are among the 2 percent of students who excelled at your studies from the very beginning, from the moment you first entered your first school the hypnotists of academia almost certainly began programming your mind, telling you that *you aren't good enough* and that *there is something wrong with you.* They taught you things like *don't get ideas above your station.* After all, they told you, there's *nothing you can do about your intelligence—you've either got it or you don't.* And even if you did well in school, *you're just not smart enough to get ahead.*

Do any of these things sound familiar? Do they sound true?

Chances are that at least one or two of them do, and I say that because I was hypnotized in exactly the same way. Fortunately, just because we have been taught that there is nothing we can do doesn't make it true. Better still, the things you are learning now will set you free to explore the larger territory of your current potential and possibilities.

What Is the Real Purpose of School?

According to the modern education expert Sir Ken Robinson, if you were an alien visiting Earth to study our education system, you would come to the conclusion that the primary purpose of education is "to produce university professors." The subjects that are valued the most, and therefore forced down the throats of most students, are those that best prepare people for a life lived in academia.

Yet the promise of school, traditionally, has been that those with higher education will go on to achieve greater economic success. If you want to better yourself in the world, the theory goes, stay longer in school before heading out into that world.

But is that still true? Has the current process of education updated itself to prepare students to live in our constantly changing and currently uncertain economic times? Even more importantly, has it helped us to tap into our true potential?

When I went to school, I was told that if I worked hard and got good grades, I would be virtually guaranteed a good job. Yet figures reveal that in the U.K., about 45 percent of recent graduates were still unemployed six months after finishing their degree.

Personally, I do not believe this to be the fault of the teachers, or the latest generation of students, or even the society in which we are living. It is simply a function of the fact that the world has shifted, and our educational system has not kept up with the changing needs of the modern world.

In other words, our school system is set up to "prepare us for life"—but the life it's designed to prepare us for disappeared in the early part of the 20th century. We now live in an information age, where the conformity encouraged by classroom dynamics can be a disadvantage, and the capacity to learn and adapt quickly is what gives us our competitive edge.

I consider myself to be an example of both the failure of the current, outmoded school system and each individual's capacity to overcome it. Our ability to learn and adapt—to get smarter—is the real competitive edge in today's society.

The Problem with Academia

I think it's fair to say, I was not the most academic of students. At first I really enjoyed school, but after a few years I found it an increasingly unhappy environment to be in. As a result, my natural interest in learning began to wane. In fact, one of my report cards said I would never amount to anything.

Now while that might destroy some people's confidence, I can be a bit stubborn. Although at some level I believed I wasn't smart enough to succeed, I went out into the world determined to be a success, if only to spite my teachers.

I worked hard, became successful in the world, and eventually earned my doctorate. When it was revealed to me that the university was licensed but not accredited, I went through the whole process again, this time earning an internationally recognized, fully accredited doctorate. And still I struggled with not feeling smart enough. When a journalist wrote an article claiming that my Ph.D. was "bogus," I felt I had to defend myself.

I got involved in a lawsuit that ran for nearly three years and nearly bankrupted me. While I eventually won the case and received substantial damages, a part of me wondered why it was so important to me that people took my degree seriously. Ultimately, I realized that my obsession with academic success was not about becoming smarter—it was about being seen as being clever.
I had gotten caught up in trying to prove something

about myself instead of simply learning more about what interested me most.

What I have learned since then is that pretty much everyone is carrying some baggage around with them about learning, and many of us originally picked this up from school. There was probably a subject you struggled with, or a teacher you didn't like, or an area in which you felt "less than." For many people, this discomfort gets logged in the unconscious mind and manifests later in life as a vague sense of anxiety about learning new things, boredom in the face of the unknown, or just a subtle, nagging feeling of doubt.

When you think about something you want or need to learn more about, if you get a feeling of apprehension, fear, or frustration, it's a sure sign that you have a learning block—something that is inhibiting your ability to smoothly take in information because the uncomfortable emotion is getting layered in with the subject itself. It's like watching a movie that has a "feeling track" as well as a soundtrack—you can't just experience it fresh because your old programs are telling you what to feel.

These blocks to learning new things strengthen the edges of our self-image and serve as "proof" that we're not smart enough to do what we really want to do or achieve what we really want to achieve. It's a bit like driving down a street with your foot on the accelerator and then suddenly slamming on the brake at random intervals. Even if we are extremely motivated to move forward, these old unconscious programs pop up when we least expect them and invisibly hold us back.

In a moment, I'm going to share a powerful technique that will help you to clear out the old baggage, blocks, fears, and frustrations of the past. By clearing out these blocks to learning, you will have more of your brain available to absorb the subject at hand and the whole subject of learning will become more and more comfortable to you. Because you'll feel more relaxed and calm, you will have more of your mind and brain available to you. This will make you smarter than before.

Setting Yourself Free

"Havening" was created by my friend Ronald Ruden, M.D., Ph.D. It is amazingly effective at relieving sadness and reducing stress, trauma, and compulsion. Dr. Ruden's work has been hailed as a remarkable breakthrough. He discovered that patterns of repeated touch to parts of the body combined with specific eye movements and visualizations have a rapid, reliable, and predictable effect on our feelings. His years of research have created a significant advance in what is known as "psychosensory therapy."

The patterns of touch used in Havening are what enable a mother to comfort her baby and they are hardwired into every infant. Havening combines these deep-rooted patterns of reassurance and comfort with sequences to break down the associations that triggered unhappy feelings. As a result, in just a few minutes we can now reduce the intensity of an emotion or feeling of stress and establish calm, robust relaxation.

This technique is not merely a distraction. It actually delinks the thought from the feeling, reducing the stress chemicals in the body, and producing states of relaxation and calm.

Even if you loved school, there are probably some experiences in your life that you wish had never happened. The effect of the specific sequence I will share with you is to clear away any old negative associations from your school years. Over time, this will actually alter the physical, neuronal pathways in your brain.

THE INSTANT BLOCK REMOVER

Read the technique all the way through before you start. You should practice this sequence of eye movements, body touches, and visualizations several times until you know it by heart. While at first it may seem a little complex, soon you will be able to use it any time you need to get rid of unhappy feelings and swiftly feel calm and relaxed.

1. Think about your experience of school or of learning in general. Notice how much stress or discomfort you are feeling and rate it on a scale of 1 to 10. This is important, as it lets you measure how much you reduce it. If your initial level of discomfort is not at least a 6 out of 10, think about additional incidents or learning situations until it is.

2. Now clear your mind, or just think about something nice.

3. Next, use both hands to tap on both your collarbones.

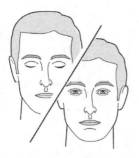

4. While you continue tapping on both your collarbones, look straight ahead, keep your head still, and close and open your eyes.

Continued

5. Continue tapping and, keeping your head still, look down to the left and then down to the right.

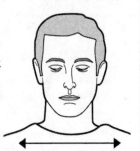

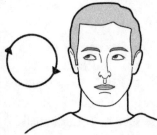

6. Continue tapping, keeping your head still, and move your eyes in a full circle clockwise and then counterclockwise.

7. Now cross your arms, place your hands on the tops of your shoulders, and close your eyes.

8. Now stroke your hands down the sides of your arms from your shoulders to your elbows, down and up, again and again.

9. As you carry on stroking the sides of your arms, imagine you are walking down a flight of stairs and count out loud from 1 to 20 with each step that you take.

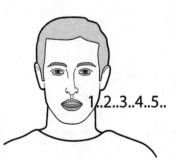

1..2..3..4..5..

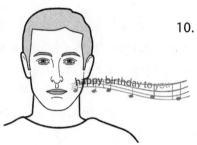

10. When you reach 20, hum "Happy Birthday."

11. Now, let your arms drop and relax them, and open your eyes and look up in front of and above you.

12. Move your eyes slowly from left to right and back three times.

13. Close your eyes and stroke the sides of your arms again five times.

14. Now open your eyes and check, on your scale from 1 to 10, the number of the feeling now.

If it is way down the bottom, congratulations—you have personally changed your own feeling state. If you think that the stressful feeling is not yet reduced enough, just repeat the sequence until it is reduced as far as you want.

IMPORTANT NOTE: This exercise is one of the most powerful in this system, and is worth repeated practice. It will work to reduce your stress and discomfort around pretty much any negative experience you can think of. If you skipped the rest of the book and just did this exercise thoroughly on each of the blocks to learning you have identified, you would become smarter!

The Power of Positive Programming

One of the most powerful examples I know of the impact of early positive programming is the story of William James Sidis, who was born in the late 19th century. His father was a Harvard professor named Boris Sidis, and as well as being a brilliant psychologist, he was also an accomplished hypnotist. Boris Sidis decided that he would put hypnosis to the test by using it to help his son become smarter.

He was successful beyond his wildest imaginings. Using little more than the power of suggestion, he taught him to tap into the innate intelligence that exists inside all of us. By the age of two, young Sidis was able to read *The New York Times*. By the age of eight, he had taught himself eight separate languages and he'd even invented his own language. Although he later rejected IQ tests, for many of the same reasons I will share with you in the next chapter, he was measured to have what is arguably the highest IQ in history.

Of course, it wasn't always smooth sailing. He was very disappointed to be denied entry into Harvard—at the age of 9. Fortunately, he didn't give up, and at the age of 11 became the youngest person ever to be admitted to the august institution.

What does this have to do with you?

If Boris Sidis could unlock his son's potential using the psychological techniques of 100 years ago, think about what's possible now using some of the cutting-edge psychological techniques you'll find in this book . . .

For example, once I recognized the pattern of childhood programming, I was able to begin to change it using the principle of hypnotic regression. Because people unconsciously act out of the patterns they learned in childhood, one of the most powerful techniques hypnotists use is to age-regress their clients to a time before the limiting pattern was created. By exposing the unconscious mind to new patterns, people are then able to create a different set of filters on what's possible.

In a moment, we are going to do a technique that many people find allows them to imagine a life beyond the limitations of their past. In your imagination, we are going to create an alternative childhood for you— one where you grew up with all the advantages of being surrounded by positive people who believed in you, believed in your potential, and had the means and the will to put those beliefs into practice.

This process will not take anything away from the childhood that you actually had, and you will not forget anything important about your past or suddenly go up to your parents and say "who are you?" It is simply a way of providing your unconscious mind with some new alternatives, which means you will no longer be constrained by the limits of your old, outdated programming.

One Important Note:

Some people had very unhappy childhoods and find it uncomfortable to think about them. Because we are imagining an alternative childhood, you do not need to think about the one you actually had to successfully complete this exercise. In fact, if you feel any discomfort during this exercise, simply stop. You can always return to it later if you choose to do so.

I am now going to ask you to close your eyes and vividly imagine having been smarter for life. The more detail you are willing to go into, the more impactful the exercise will be. Keep experimenting with it until you really get a strong sense of exactly what it would have been like . . .

YOUR SMARTER CHILDHOOD

Read the technique all the way through before you start, so you know exactly what to do. Then, when you're ready, go back through really taking the time to imagine the following scenario in great detail.

Imagine being born into a wonderful home where from the moment you enter the world, you absolutely know that you are loved, you are wanted, and you are supported in whatever it is you want to do—a truly smart environment.

What is it like to be a small child knowing that wherever you go and whatever you do, you are loved, wanted, and supported? What kinds of things are you interested in? What are you curious about? What kinds of positive messages and advice do you receive in this smart environment? What kinds of beliefs do you form about what's possible growing up in this smarter world?

What would it be like to be a teenager having grown up knowing from the moment you were born that you were smart enough to do whatever you truly wanted to do? What kinds of things would you want to study? What would you want to learn? What kinds of hopes and dreams might you have for your future? How secure and confident do you feel?

Continued

How about as you are making the transition to adulthood—what kinds of things do you want to do? Who do you want to do them with? What do you choose to learn and practice? How do you feel about yourself? How do you feel about life, knowing that you are smart enough to do anything you truly want to do?

Where does your curiosity take you in your 20s?
In your 30s?
In your 40s?
In your 50s?
In your 60s?
In your 70s?

What is it like to grow old having spent a lifetime knowing that you were loved, wanted, and have always been smart enough to do whatever you wanted to do? What are some of the most wonderful things that you have learned?

Take your time to really enjoy and explore this alternative life path. When you are ready, you can return to now, feeling refreshed and alert and knowing that everything you've learned is yours to keep . . .

Each time you repeat this exercise, you will uncover new possibilities. You will begin to feel more comfortable following your curiosity in a variety of situations. Before you know it, you will begin to experience tangible changes in how you approach learning new things at school or work and in your life.

You can reinforce these learnings each time you listen to the hypnotic trance . . .

In the next chapter, we'll look at one of the most common reasons people give me for their learning difficulties—an inability to concentrate. I'll share some cutting-edge research and personal experiences that will demonstrate to you that there are effective alternatives to drug-based treatments for concentration difficulties. Finally, we'll create a different kind of anchor for concentration that will enable you to concentrate just the right amount for whatever the task at hand . . .

THE WHOLE CHAPTER IN ONE PAGE

- For better and for worse, our parents and teachers were powerful hypnotists.

- Schools were not designed to make you smarter—they were designed to prepare you for life in an industrial society that is no longer prevalent in much of the world.

- Many brilliant people think they are not because they have been judged against a particular view of the mind that thinks academic conformity is more important than real-world success.

- Pretty much everyone is carrying some baggage around with them about learning. You can reduce that baggage and open your mind back up to learning through the process known as "Havening."

- You have massive potential.

- It's never too late to have a smarter childhood.

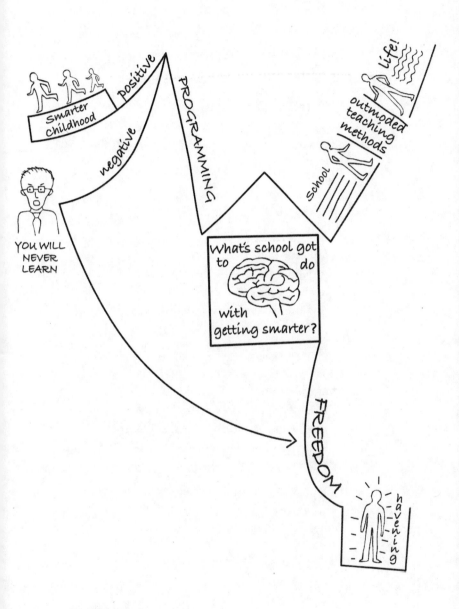

GET INTO THE ZONE!

Before you begin to read this chapter, check in to see if you are in your learning zone. If not, follow the steps below:

1. Take three slow and gentle breaths. Allow your body to relax and feel good.

2. Squeeze your thumb and middle finger together, firing off your "natural learning" anchor until you can begin to feel yourself going into a relaxed state of absorbed fascination.

3. Now, imagine what you would look like if you were just a little bit smarter than you are right now. How would you sit? What kind of expression would you have on your face? How would that smarter you show up in the world? How would they smile and interact with other people?

4. Step into that smarter you so that you're seeing what they see, hearing what they hear, and feeling the way they feel.

When you are ready, begin . . .

•

CHAPTER 4

The Easy Way to Boost Your Concentration

One of the Most Exclusive Clubs in the World

Imagine being invited to join a club whose membership is drawn from some of the greatest minds from throughout history. Here are just a few of its members:

Charlotte Brontë

Emily Brontë

Lord Byron

Winston Churchill

Christopher Columbus

Billy Connolly

Salvador Dalí

Emily Dickinson

Thomas Edison

Albert Einstein

Malcolm Forbes

Henry Ford

John F. Kennedy

Wolfgang Amadeus Mozart

George Orwell

Pablo Picasso

Sir Walter Raleigh

Mark Twain

Virginia Woolf

William Butler Yeats

What binds these geniuses and success stories to-gether? They have all exhibited symptoms of or been for-mally diagnosed with attention-deficit disorder (ADD) or attention-deficit/hyperactivity disorder (ADHD). I too am an unofficial member of this worthy club. Yet for me, the same "inability to concentrate" that seemed such a problem to my teachers at school has been one of the keys to my success.

Because my mind seems to run at a faster speed than many other people's, I've learned to use it differ-ently. For example, while some people say multitasking is a myth, I can concentrate on several things simulta-neously. This was actually a prerequisite of some of the jobs I've done in the past as a radio DJ and in my stage hypnotism show, both of which required me to split my attention in many different ways.

A Hunter in a Farmer's World

One of the most interesting researchers I've met in the field of ADD/ADHD is Thom Hartmann. One of the ideas he is famous for is that ADD is more of an evolutionary problem than an individual one. According to Hartmann, ADD isn't a disease, and it doesn't mean someone is broken—it's simply another way of being in the world, one that is very well suited to the more "high adrenaline" professions like entrepreneurship, live performance, and the practice of emergency medicine, but poorly suited to a traditional school setting.

To better understand his theory, think about the two types of society that existed long ago. There were hunter-gatherers, whose survival was dependent on being able to catch live food and forage effectively, and there were farmers, whose survival was dependent on being able to cultivate the land and grow food over time. To be an effective farmer, you needed to cultivate patience, consistency, and a long-term view for decision-making. To be an effective hunter, you needed to cultivate constant shifts in attention (so you can spot potential prey), lightning-fast decision-making (so you can decide between chasing after the deer or the rabbit), and a high degree of flexibility, so you could adapt to the constantly changing migration patterns of animal behavior.

Now imagine that the hunter and farmer are forced to trade places for a month. The same qualities that were virtues in one context would prove disastrous in the other. The farmer's long-term consistency would prove too inflexible in the forests and jungles of the hunter; the hunter's impulsivity would destroy the farm. It's not that the fast-twitch thought process of the hunter is better or worse than the slow-twitch thinking of the farmer—it's just that they each work well in the environments for which they are suited, but would appear as dysfunctions in a different kind of environment.

I grew up in a world with three television channels and no Internet. Today, there are over 400 TV channels and the infinite variety of the Internet. We are living in the most stimulating time in history, so of course people are going to need to adapt and learn to apply their intelligence to multiple inputs simultaneously. In this sense, much of what we consider to be "learning difficulties" may actually be early adaptations to environmental changes taking place in the world.

For example, children today are often accused of having a short or even nonexistent attention span. But there is no evidence suggesting any real difference in attention capacity between this generation and previous generations—it's simply that kids growing up with all the different types of stimulation and information sources available today have had to adapt to the modern world by flicking through those information sources more effectively. And recent research has shown that once they find what they want and need, they're able to concentrate on it as well as anyone else. Far from being a problem, this newly developed "hypersearch" capability is a necessary asset for our modern world.

The Two Types of Concentration

We all know how to concentrate—it's a natural human ability. You can notice this the next time you go to the supermarket. Some people are concentrating on what they are doing, using a kind of active, engaged concentration to pick out the exact tomato or cut of meat they want. Others can be found with a can of beans in one hand and a can of soup in the other, staring off into space, concentrating on whatever it is they're thinking about.

The same thing is true when people drive. Some concentrate actively on the task at hand, whereas others let their unconscious do most of the driving while they concentrate on enjoying the scenery, a conversation with a passenger, or something they've been thinking about. The only problem arises if you allow your concentration to wander too far away from the task at hand. This is why it's extremely useful to get a better understanding of the two different types of concentration.

Active concentration is when you're really focused on the task at hand, eyes wide open, sitting forward, intensely involved in whatever it is that you're doing. It is the type of concentration that is particularly useful for performance, whether that performance is on a playing field, in a boardroom, or during an examination.

The tennis champions Jim Courier and Greg Rusedski both used my hypnotic techniques at various stages of their careers. In 1999 they ended up playing against each other in the Davis Cup and the match was held in England. Every time Greg scored a point, the crowd would go wild; when Jim scored a point, there was hardly any noise from the crowd at all.

As it happened Jim won the match, and in the interview immediately afterwards he was asked how it felt to have the crowd against him in such a loud and obvious way. He looked a bit surprised and said, "I didn't really notice the crowd." That is a great example of the power of an intense state of focus and active concentration.

Similarly, I once treated a leading surgeon for stress. He was concerned that he would be too distracted by what was going on in his life at that time to go into a state of deep hypnosis. I asked him if there was any area of his life where he was able to stay really focused on the task at hand, regardless of what else might be going on in his life.

He replied, "Certainly, when I'm doing an operation."

And I said, "So, if I dropped something next to you, like a scalpel, would it make you jump?"

He replied, "Of course not."

So I asked him to remember in vivid detail the last one of these operations that he'd done. I saw his eyes defocus and concentrate on the images that he was creating in his mind to the exclusion of everything else, thereby re-creating that quality of active concentration while his body remained in a relaxed state.

Passive concentration, on the other hand, is when you sit back and relax and allow things to come to you. You are fully absorbed by the experience, but there is no active effort to engage with it.

Anytime you've been engrossed in a movie, a sporting event, or even just listening to music or an interesting conversation, you were using your passive concentration. Even though you weren't making any effort to remember what happened, often you can recall many small details of what happened and what was said, including any moments you found funny or moving.

When we use our passive concentration, we're taking everything in, but we're not *trying* to take it in. If we're watching a romantic story, we can feel the romance. When things get exciting, we get excited as well. Some people would even say they weren't concentrating at all—they were simply engrossed by what was happening and because of that quality of attention, they actually picked up more than someone who was trying to take notes and analyze the story.

So, some things will be easier to do in a state of active concentration; others will be easier in a state of passive concentration. Yet many people have become habituated to one kind of concentration over the other, and either stay too amped up and hyperfocused to really absorb new information or too passive to put it to use.

This next exercise will put the power back into your hands, allowing you to actively choose which kind of concentration you use at what time. As with all the exercises in this book, it will get easier to do each time you do it, and will be reinforced and strengthened each time you use the hypnotic trances.

How to Take Control of Your Concentration

Have you ever seen a mixing board? It's a collection of knobs and sliders designed to let a music producer create an optimal mix between all the different sounds being recorded. Each slider goes from zero to ten, like the volume control on a stereo. This allows the producer to make simple, smooth adjustments as needed during the actual recording.

We are going to use this same system to create a slider in your mind—one that will enable you to effortlessly slide between active and passive concentration so that you are always concentrating appropriately for the task at hand.

So imagine that there is a slider in your mind that looks like this:

On the left-hand side, you have passive concentration—your ability to simply relax and absorb information without any active involvement from your conscious mind. On the right, you have active concentration—your ability to fully engage your mind and, where necessary, your body, in the task at hand.

By installing this slider in your mind, it will train your neurology and physiology to be able to quickly and literally switch from one state to another state. Now, this is very useful, because then we have much more control over our thoughts and our feelings and our states and once we control our state, we control our behaviors, and then we have a much more powerful impact upon the way we affect the world.

THE CONCENTRATION SLIDER, PART ONE

Read the technique all the way through before you start.

1. Remember a time when you were in a state of passive concentration—watching a TV show, listening to music, or any time that you were relaxed and absorbed by what was going on around you without any effort at all.

2. Return to that time as though you were back there again now. See what you saw, hear what you heard, and feel how you felt. As you do, make sure your concentration slider is all the way to the **left**.

3. Go back through this memory at least three more times with the slider all the way to the **left**.

4. Now, remember a time that you were in a state of active concentration. Perhaps it was a time where you were really sitting forward, fully engaged, using all of your attention to take in as much as you could. Your energy was up, you had a little bit of an adrenaline kick, and you were fully engaged.

5. Return to that time as though you were back there. See what you saw, hear what you heard, and feel how you felt. This time, make sure your concentration slider is all the way to the **right**.

6. Go back through this memory at least three more times with the slider all the way to the **right.**

7. Now gently move the slider back over to the **left** and think of another time where you have been relaxed and absorbed in a state of passive concentration.

8. Now gently move the slider back over to the **right** and think of another time where you were fully engaged in a state of active concentration.

9. Repeat this back-and-forth movement of the slider at least three more times, being sure to stop at the far left and far right long enough to remember at least one specific incident of passive concentration on the left and one specific incident of active concentration when the slider is on the right.

Now that we have set up your concentration slider, we are going to take things one step further to give you even more control over your concentration . . .

THE CONCENTRATION SLIDER, PART TWO

Read the technique all the way through before you start.

1. When you're ready, slide your concentration slider all the way to the **left** and enjoy the feeling of relaxed, passive concentration.

2. Now, move your slider just a little bit to the **right**, slowly enough so that a little bit of active concentration begins to come into the mix. First 10 percent, then 20 percent, then 30 percent . . . Continue to move the slider slowly to the **right** so that the two concentrations gently mix.

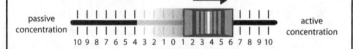

3. As the slider moves, you start to feel a 50/50 mix of passive and active concentration, like a special effect in a movie when one scene slowly dissolves into another. As you move your concentration slider more towards the **right**, the passive concentration fades out completely and the active concentration fades in.

4. When you get all the way to the right, slowly move the slider back the other way. Notice the active concentration fade out as the slider moves back to the middle, and then the passive concentration come up more and more as the slider continues over to the **left**.

passive concentration

active concentration

5. Repeat this process at least five times, sliding from left to right (passive to active) and then back from right to left (active to passive). Do it again and again until you can feel your concentration shifting in sync with the slider in your mind.

You now have a greater degree of control over your concentration, so that you can boost your levels of active or passive concentration in any situation and at any time!

Once you've practiced this technique a number of times, you will be able to do it automatically simply by thinking about it. It will be reinforced each time you listen to the "Smarter While You Sleep" hypnotic trance, and we will incorporate it into the "Get into the Zone" section at the beginning of each chapter until it becomes second nature to you.

In the next chapter, we'll take a look at what "genius" really means and how you can get the most out of what you already have. Until then, take a few moments to review the key ideas from this chapter and the mind map that follows . . .

THE WHOLE CHAPTER IN ONE PAGE

- Many of the most successful and creative people throughout history have experienced symptoms currently associated with ADD and ADHD.

- Different patterns of attention may have evolved from the varying needs of society over time. Each pattern of attention is designed to work well within the particular society from which it evolved.

- There are two types of concentration—active and passive. Active concentration is high energy and is ideal for performance-type activities. Passive concentration is more relaxed, and allows for a bigger-picture absorption of what's really going on.

- You can choose which kind of concentration to bring to each major task throughout your day.

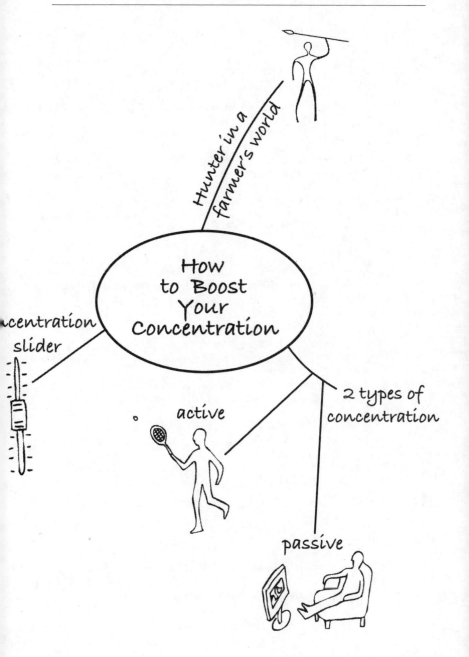

GET INTO THE ZONE!

Before you begin to read this chapter, check in to see if you are in your learning zone. If not, follow the steps below:

1. Take three slow and gentle breaths. Allow your body to relax and feel good.

2. Squeeze your thumb and middle finger together, firing off your "natural learning" anchor until you can begin to feel yourself going into a relaxed state of absorbed fascination.

3. Now, imagine what you would look like if you were just a little bit smarter than you are right now. How would you sit? What kind of expression would you have on your face? How would that smarter you show up in the world? How would they smile and interact with other people?

4. Step into that smarter you so that you're seeing what they see, hearing what they hear, and feeling the way they feel.

5. Set your concentration slider to the perfect blend of passive and active attention.

When you are ready, begin . . .

CHAPTER 5

•

Unleash Your Inner Genius

Understanding IQ

In the early 1900s, a man named Alfred Binet was tasked with developing a test that would compare children's mental abilities relative to their peers. The test evolved over time and was soon adopted by Stanford University, quickly becoming the gold standard for measuring intelligence. To this day the Stanford-Binet IQ test is the primary one used around the world to assess people's quotient, or capacity, for intelligence.

Yet far from it being designed as a measure of intelligence as an innate character trait, Alfred Binet created the original tests as an early-warning system to identify students who would need extra support at school. The hope was that early detection of problems would help ensure that everyone got a fair chance to succeed. He even went so far as to warn that scores should not be interpreted literally as measures of potential, due to the "plasticity" of intelligence.

What is plasticity? While we will talk about this in more depth later in the book, plasticity is a way of describing the extraordinary adaptive capacity of the human brain. Throughout our lives, our brain continues to evolve, depending on how we use it.

For example, it's a common belief that chess grandmasters must be more intelligent than the rest of us, and that they perhaps even had a genetic predisposition towards chess mastery. But studies have shown that despite their extraordinary abilities, the only bit of a chess master's brain that's different from yours or mine is the

[handwritten margin note:] "Just be he thought / believed that doesn't mean he was correct, what's the truth?"

specific bit that has to do with playing chess—and that develops *after* they start playing, not before. Contrary to many of the stories told to us by the popular press, we can continue to get smarter throughout our lives, no matter how old we are or how old we get.

Alfred Binet intuited this years before the scientific equipment was available for running tests that now demonstrate it. In fact, to him it was just common sense. So if the man who created the model for modern IQ tests was smart enough to know that our actual capacity for intelligence is not measurable, then perhaps we can all learn something truly valuable from our IQ score—that we can never accurately measure our future possibilities on the basis of our current reality.

Multiple Intelligences

Most of us have been taught to think that we are either intelligent or we are not. But the definitions of intelligence we learned at school were built around the specific types of intelligence that are most valued at school—verbal intelligence, which is a measure of our ability to learn and use languages to reach goals and be effective in the world, and logical/numerical intelligence, which is a measure of our ability to analyze problems logically and scientifically and carry out mathematical operations.

Researchers into the field of intelligence have identified as many as ten separate intelligences, of which only a few are measured in the standardized IQ tests that serve as the basis of so much of what we in our culture think of as "intelligent."

Here are the seven most commonly agreed upon intelligences, along with a short description of what skills they refer to and some of the common professions that take full advantage of them. As you read, notice which of these intelligences are most developed in you and which you feel are currently your weakest:

1. **Verbal Intelligence**—your ability to express yourself through language
   Examples: Writer, Teacher, Speaker

2. **Logical/Numerical Intelligence**—your ability to analyze problems logically, investigate them scientifically, or solve them mathematically
   Examples: Scientist, Accountant, Professor

3. **Emotional Intelligence**—your ability to understand the intentions, motivations, and desires of others and to appreciate your own feelings, fears, and motivations. (This is the classic "street smart" vs. "book smart")
   Examples: Policeman, Counselor, Parent

4. **Body/Kinesthetic Intelligence**—your ability to use your whole body to create results; the ability to use mental skills to coordinate bodily movements
   Examples: Athlete, Sculptor, Dancer

5. **Spatial Intelligence**—your ability to recognize and use patterns of wide space and more confined areas
   Examples: Architect, Interior designer, Artist

6. **Creative Intelligence**—your ability to create new things and partake in "the radiant, explosive thought process that leads one into new realms of thinking and expression"
   Examples: Inventor, Innovator, Writer, Musician

7. **Spiritual Intelligence**—our ability to understand how we fit together into the larger picture of life, and how we recognize and adapt to our role as individuals and as a species in the universe
   Examples: Thought leader in any field, religious or otherwise

Each of us currently has a unique blend of intelligences. By reading and applying what you will learn in this book, you will be able not only to increase your capacity within one or more of these intelligences, but you will also discover how best to take advantage of the uniqueness of your own current configuration of intelligences.

Throughout this book we will primarily be focusing on helping you to get smarter by developing your verbal, logical/numerical, emotional, creative, and spiritual intelligences. This is not to devalue either spatial or body/kinesthetic intelligence—simply a recognition of the fact that a book is not the ideal forum to learn more about the properties of the physical world. However, the hypnotic trances will in fact also help you to evolve all seven of these critical intelligences for life.

The Myth of Talent

Is David Beckham a genius? When it comes to bending a football around a wall of people intent on stopping it, I can't think of a better word for it. After all, how many people do you know that had a movie named after the unique abilities of their right foot?

When I had the chance to ask him whether he thought his physics-defying kicks were the result of some innate talent, he laughed and told me the story of how he used to practice for hours and hours, kicking thousands of soccer balls around various configurations of trees and furniture in his backyard.

Dr. Daniel Levitin is the researcher behind the increasingly well-known research into the amount of practice it takes to achieve world-class expert status in whatever field you happen to be involved in.

In Levitin's own words:

> . . . ten thousand hours of practice is required to achieve the level of mastery associated with being a world-class expert—in anything. In study after study, of composers, basketball players, fiction writers, ice skaters, concert pianists, chess players, master criminals, and what have you, this number comes up again and again. Ten thousand hours is the equivalent to roughly three hours per day, or twenty hours per week, of practice over ten years . . . It seems that it takes the brain this long to assimilate all that it needs to know to achieve true mastery.

So when someone tells me "I can't draw well," or "I'm no good at sports," or "I'm not a natural writer," I invariably ask them, "How many hours have you spent practicing?" It is very rare indeed that the answer is anywhere near 100 hours, let alone 10,000. The implication is that their apparent lack of skill is usually less a function of a lack of innate talent than it is a reflection of a lack of time and effort spent on the outside.

Of course you don't need to be brilliant at everything to have a wonderful life. Indeed, people who have hyperdeveloped one or more of the intelligences have often done so at the cost of some of the others. We all know of people who excel in their careers but struggle in their personal lives.

But what is heartening is to know that almost anything you would like to excel at will succumb to an investment of time and what psychologists call "deep practice"—continual focused effort with constant feedback that allows you to adjust and learn as you go. While it won't turn a one-legged man into the next David Beckham, it can easily allow you to excel at what you want to do most, until the people around you say, "You are a genius at that!"

PUTTING IN THE HOURS

1. Think of a complex skill you have mastered in the course of your lifetime.
    Example: Playing skills (chess, a musical instrument, or a sport); Work-related skills (coaching, teaching, brain surgery, etc.); Language skills (French, Russian, HTML, etc.)

2. Make a "best guess" as to how many hours you put in between your initial interest in the skill and your relative mastery of it. Over what period of time did you put in those hours?
    Example: 250 hours over one year, 100 hours over eight years, 1,000 hours in three months, etc.

3. Now, choose a skill or project that you are currently working on, and make a "best guess" as to how many hours you have put into it so far, and how many more hours you will need to put in to get where you want to go.
    Example: I've put in 60 hours so far; I probably need to spend at least that much time again to get to the level I want to reach.

4. By when would you like to have completed your new project or mastered your new skill?

    A simple calculation will tell you how many hours you need to put in each day, week, month, or year to get where you want to go in the time frame you want to get there.

The Four Stages of Mastery

When people first begin to learn something new, they often underestimate what it will really take to succeed. This is the stage of **unconscious incompetence**, where you do not yet know what you don't yet know.

When at some point you try it for yourself and begin to discover how close to the beginning of the learning curve you actually are, you enter the stage of **conscious incompetence**. You are regularly making mistakes, and frustration and confusion are your regular companions. What will keep you going through this stage is both the recognition that it is simply a necessary step in the learning process and the cultivation of a state of sincere determination.

The reason most people don't get further along in their practice is that they mistake the conscious incompetence stage of the learning process as an actual inability to learn or perform. But by redoubling their efforts and learning from their mistakes, they will break through.

A few years back, the comedy actor David Walliams came to see me to help him prepare for his 20-mile swim across the English Channel. He knew that the combination of the distance and the cold meant that he would inevitably slide into states of frustration and fatigue at some point during his swim. So I asked him to remember times in his life where he had exhibited tenacious resolve and a strong determination to succeed. As he repeatedly went into these states of powerful determination, we anchored them to automatically come up whenever he started to flag during his swim.

In a moment, I am going to do the same thing with you. We are going to build a superstate of determination and program your mind to go into that state whenever the going gets tough in your own learning. Instead of giving up, you too will be able to redouble your efforts and continue your practice until you move into the stage of **conscious competence**.

At this point in the learning cycle, you know *how* to do something but you can only successfully do it with your full, conscious attention. You may still need checklists or carefully followed "recipes" to successfully demonstrate your learning, but continued conscious practice leads to automation of the learning, which in turn leads to the stage of **unconscious competence**.

This is the ultimate goal of most learning and skill development—the point at which you have so much practice under your belt that what you have been learning has become "second nature" to you.

To get the most out of this next technique, think of a specific subject you would like to learn or skill you would like to master . . .

DETERMINED TO SUCCEED

Read the technique all the way through before you start.

1. Put your attention on the spot between your eyebrows and remember a time when you felt determined and thought, "I'm just going to do it!" It might be in relation to a cause you feel strongly about, a goal you are committed to achieving, or something you felt driven to accomplish against the odds.

2. Return to that memory like you are back there again now. See what you saw, hear what you heard, and feel how you felt.

3. Now make the colors richer and brighter, the sounds louder, and the feelings stronger.

4. Squeeze your thumb and little finger on your right hand together and create an associational link between the feeling of determination and your finger squeeze as you run through the memory of determination at least three more times.

5. Now, squeeze your thumb and little finger together and imagine the subject or skill that you want to master. See yourself facing challenges and even making mistakes but, instead of frustration, you feel these increased feelings of determination and motivation to succeed.

6. Repeat this process at least five more times until you only have to think about a challenge to feel the determination to resolve it!

A Quick Look Ahead . . .

In this first section of the book, you have learned that getting smarter is the natural result of learning to use more of your brain and more of your mind in everything you do. You have also seen that the only three things that determine your success or failure in whatever it is you want to learn are the state you are in, the strategy you are using, and the amount of practice you are willing to put in.

You have cleared any blocks that may have arisen from early negative experiences around school or learning, and begun to see yourself as smarter than before. You have created a slider in your mind that you can use to easily boost your levels of passive and active concentration. Finally, we have explored the many different intelligences available to all of us, and seen how our capacity to express any given intelligence has more to do with the hours of practice we put in than with any innate ability or social advantage we have been born with. Take a few moments to review the key ideas from this chapter and the mind map on the following pages before moving into Section II of this book, where you will learn "A Smarter Way to Learn" . . .

THE WHOLE CHAPTER IN ONE PAGE

- IQ tests were designed to measure someone's current skill level, not their innate capacity for learning.

- There are many intelligences, although in school we have learned to focus primarily on language skills and mathematical, sequential thinking.

- Life is made up primarily of skills that can be learned, not abilities or talents that we are born with. By recognizing this fact and approaching learning new things accordingly, you will find yourself able to learn and grow even in areas that you had previously thought were beyond you.

- You have not even begun to tap into your true potential.

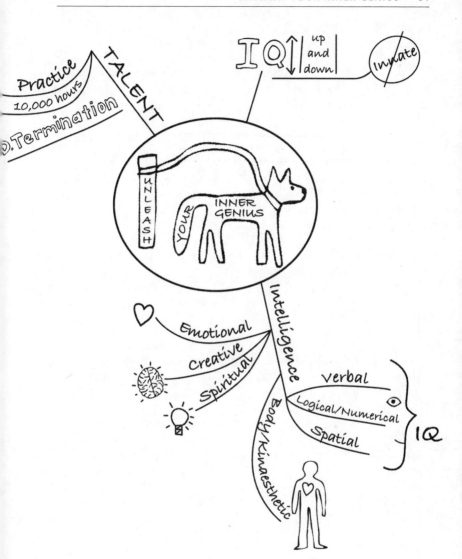

SECTION II

A SMARTER WAY
TO LEARN

In Section II of this book, you will learn how to spend more and more time in your optimal learning state—the boundless desire and enthusiasm for new information and new possibilities that came to you so naturally as a child and is still there inside you, waiting to be reawakened.

If you're in school, or in fact if you're a student of pretty much anything at any age, I'll show you how to master the basics like reading and note taking and math and spelling, things you've almost certainly been taught but may never have learned properly.

We'll also explore the mysterious world of memory, and you'll learn some simple strategies that will enable you to remember more of what you learn and reliably access the information you need in the situations in which you most need it.

By the time we're done, you'll be able to learn with ease, study effectively, and approach your exams with confidence!

GET INTO THE ZONE!

Before you begin to read this chapter, check in to see if you are in your learning zone. If not, follow the steps below:

1. Take three slow and gentle breaths. Allow your body to relax and feel good.

2. Squeeze your thumb and middle finger together, firing off your "natural learning" anchor until you can begin to feel yourself going into a relaxed state of absorbed fascination.

3. Now, imagine what you would look like if you were just a little bit smarter than you are right now. How would you sit? What kind of expression would you have on your face? How would that smarter you show up in the world? How would they smile and interact with other people?

4. Step into that smarter you so that you're seeing what they see, hearing what they hear, and feeling the way they feel.

5. Set your concentration slider to the perfect blend of passive and active attention.

When you are ready, begin . . .

CHAPTER 6

•

Accelerating the
Learning Curve

The Three Levels of Learning

What's something you'd love to learn?

Is it a subject, like geography, math, science, or history?

A social skill, like speaking with confidence or making friends quickly and easily?

How about learning a new language, or the customs of a country you've never been to before?

Whatever your answer, here's the most important thing you need to know before you begin:

To what level do you want to learn it?

Essentially, there are three different levels we can learn at. The first level is information—we simply want to get some new information into our heads for the purpose of repeating it back or putting it to use later (say, in a school exam). This is the level of learning we might pursue if we are studying for trivia night or for an exam in a subject we are required to take but have no interest in or intention of ever using again.

If your goal is just the input and output of information, the memory strategies in Chapter 8 will serve you well. But if you want to go deeper than the mere parroting of facts and figures, the second level of learning goes beyond information to a deeper understanding of the subject you are learning.

For example, I have always been fascinated by hypnosis and the workings of the human mind. Although

I've never had to take any sort of formal exam on the subject, my interest is intense enough that I wanted to gain a real understanding of how the mind works. This understanding is useful, but it is also its own reward.

Finally, sometimes your primary goal in learning is application—that is, you want to be able to put what you are learning into practice in the world. Whether you are learning how to drive, operate a computer, or do brain surgery, when your goal is application, the proof is in the pudding. You know you've learned successfully when you can do whatever it is you learned to do.

While you may well want to learn something at all three levels in order to optimize your learning, once you identify which level you want to learn at, you will know which strategies to use.

- *For **gathering information**, use the reading, note taking, and memory strategies from throughout Section II.*

- *For gaining **deeper understanding**, use the chunking and mind-mapping tools in this chapter to break down even the most complex subjects into easy-to-manage, simple-to-understand bite-size chunks.*

- *When your ultimate goal is the **real-world application** of what you are studying, you can accelerate your learning curve and surprise yourself by applying the natural learning strategies from the fields of NLP and Behavioral Modeling that I will share with you later in this chapter.*

Over the rest of this chapter, I will introduce you to two of the core strategies for learning and two amazing techniques you can learn in just a few minutes that will dramatically increase the speed and effectiveness of your learning.

How Do You Eat an Elephant?

In the early 1980s, Dr. Richard Bandler, the co-creator of the field of Neuro-Linguistic Programming (NLP), was brought in by the American army to improve their pistol shooting. Prior to Dr. Bandler's arrival on the scene, pistol training consisted of handing each of the soldiers a gun, showing them how to hold and aim it, and then having them shoot at a target nearly 100 feet away. Some soldiers could hit the target from the very beginning, but many others only improved a small amount from beginning to end of the training. The assumption was that some soldiers were innately talented at shooting while others were not. Yet nothing could have been further from the truth.

What Dr. Bandler did was change the program so all the soldiers began by shooting at the target from only ten feet away. When they could consistently hit that target, they would shoot at targets 20 feet away, then 30 feet, then 40 feet, and so on down the line until they could consistently hit a target at 100 feet away. This simple change in their learning strategy led to a significant improvement in their level of results.

The principle behind what Dr. Bandler did is called "chunking down"—the breaking down of a subject or task into small enough chunks that they can easily be learned and mastered before moving on, and then reassembling those chunks until the entire subject or task has been learned.

Now, in the same way, you can learn anything, no matter how complex, if you first take the time to break the task down into small enough chunks for you to understand and master.

One of my favorite examples of the power of chunking came when I was working with my friend the actor Dougray Scott. He was due to appear in the West End in the title role of the play *Beckett*, which is over three hours long and had more dialogue in it than any part he had previously been called on to play. He asked me if I would help him to prepare.

In order to make the task seem less daunting, I asked Dougray to divide the play into four and tell me the gist of what each quarter was about. I then had him divide each quarter into individual scenes and to describe each scene in his own words. Before long, we had broken the entire play down into a series of easily learnable chunks. Within a few weeks, he had learned the entire part.

Seeing the Forest for the Trees

Of course, sometimes the problem is exactly the opposite—we can get caught up in the details of something and lose sight of the big picture.

When the business entrepreneur Peter Jones was doing his TV show *Tycoon*, he sent a man called Justin Chieffo, who'd invented a new kind of shopping bag, to see me. He was so enthusiastic about his product that he wanted people to know every detail of how it worked, from how it was manufactured to where the materials were sourced to how he thought the bags would best be sold. I was impressed, but also overloaded with information and unnecessary details.

So I said to him, "Look, this is all very good, but you need to grab my attention if you're going in to see these supermarkets. What's unique about these bags? What's amazing? What's really brilliant about this?"

He stopped to think for a few moments, then replied, "Well, I suppose if it worked, it would change the world."

I told him to walk into meetings and open with the big chunk line, "The idea I'm about to share with you will revolutionize the retail industry." And not only did he sell his bags to a lot of people, he did help revolutionize the industry.

The strategy we used in this instance is called "chunking up." To do this for yourself, take a number of seemingly separate ideas and find the common theme or essence that unites them. You can then continue to chunk up until you are left with one simple idea that encompasses all of the smaller ones.

Mind Mapping

The single best process I know for putting chunking into action as a part of your own learning strategies is called "mind mapping." Originally developed by the brilliant learning expert Tony Buzan, mind mapping combines chunking with whole-brain learning to create one of the most comprehensive and enjoyable learning tools available.

I used mind mapping throughout the process of writing this book, and you've already seen a number of examples of mind maps at the end of each chapter. By combining words and imagery in a simple weblike drawing, you create new connections between the left and the right brains, allowing you both to learn information more easily and to output it more effectively.

Traditional note taking involves writing down everything that an author or teacher is saying in a linear, sequential fashion. Afterwards, you are left to review your notes in the same order and sequence that you originally made them. But mind mapping uses chunking to create a sort of a hierarchical map. At the very center is the "big idea"; then the big idea is divided into smaller and smaller chunks like branches of a tree all growing out of the same solid trunk.

This mirrors the way the brain actually records information. As we will discuss later in the chapter on memory, our brains don't store things sequentially like in a filing cabinet—ideas are held together by a network of abstract associations called neural networks, allowing us to branch out from a central idea to other, connected ideas.

Here are some guidelines you can use to begin creating mind maps to gain a deeper understanding of anything you want to learn more about:

1. **Begin with the central idea.**

2. **Create branches off this central idea.**

3. **Break each of the main branches down into smaller branches. Continue until you've got the whole chapter represented on one page.**

4. **Create an image to go with each key idea, or chunk. The images don't need to look good in order to be effective. It's in the act of creating each image for yourself that your brain makes new connections, and information turns to understanding.**

On the following page you will see two different examples of the mind maps of Chapter 4. Remember that mind mapping is not about artistic ability, it's about creating a link between left and right brain using images and words to help you easily remember and understand whatever you are learning.

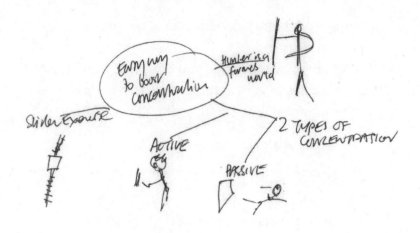

CALL TO ACTION

Create your own mind maps

Go back through the book and create your own mind maps for each of the chapters. Don't worry if they look different from the ones I have provided. The simple act of drawing your own mind map will not only ensure that you will learn the material at a deeper level, it will also make it easier to recall the key ideas and put them into action in your life.

Natural Learning

The "master strategy" we are continually taught to use in school is simple repetition. While this is an effective way of mastering certain core skills, like addition and multiplication, it is a terrible strategy for most things we want to understand and apply.

By way of contrast, think about how people learn to drive cars. For years before we ever get behind the steering wheel of a car, we sit and watch Mom and Dad and all sorts of different people drive and we see how it's done. For most people, by the time they finally get behind the wheel for themselves, they have seen the process so many times that they are able to quickly grasp the skill with a minimal amount of instruction.

But if we learned to drive a car the way we learned things at school, it would be done like this—this is a nut, this is a bolt, this is another nut, this is a bolt, this is a wheel, this is another wheel, this is a crankshaft, this is an engine. Years, perhaps even decades later we might have an understanding of what a car is and how it works, but we still would be no closer to being able to drive it than we were on day one.

So when your primary goal is the application of what you have learned in the form of a new or advanced level of skill, the simplest strategy is to observe someone who is already excellent at that skill until we are ready to copy it.

For example, years ago I had the chance to appear on the British TV series *Top Gear* and drive the "Reasonably

Priced Car" around the track. Although I wasn't a particularly good driver, I was fiercely competitive, so I decided to apply the natural learning strategy to see how quickly I could get better.

So I asked a model of excellence—in this case the character known as the "Stig"—if I could watch him drive around the track several times from inside the car. I paid particular attention to the details of what he did—when he put his foot to the floor, how hard and how often he braked, and how far he spun the steering wheel around when he took the turns.

As well as watching what was going on in his body, I asked him some questions to get insights into what was going on in his mind. I wanted to know how he knew when to speed up and slow down, and in particular how he knew when to begin his turns and when to accelerate out of them.

Finally, I used the mind-programming technique I am about to share with you to mentally rehearse the drive. I watched him race the track in my mind's eye, and then imagined being him, stepping into the car and seeing the track through his eyes. One of the things I noticed when I was "being" him was that I could see a little curve in my mind that represented the line to take around the track.

By the time I actually stepped into the car, I had already driven the race dozens of times in my mind. Afterwards, the Stig commented on how quickly I had picked up the handling of the car and the track. This was not because of any special driving ability I had, but simply because of the effectiveness of the strategy I used to learn.

This process, which in NLP is called "Modeling," is something you can use to accelerate your learning curve with almost any skill you can imagine. Simply by watching what someone excellent at the skill does and moving our body in the same way, we can shortcut the learning process. The unconscious learns through immersion and absorption, so each time we repeat the process we are creating a new muscle memory that will then be available to us when we need it. Surprisingly often, we gain insights into the expert's thought process as well.

In hypnosis, this process is called "deep-trance identification"—but you can get many of the same effects by simply doing the following exercise.

MODELING EXCELLENCE

Read the technique all the way through before you start.

1. Choose a skill you would like to learn or master. Identify someone who is a model of excellence for that skill.

2. Spend as much time as you can studying that person in action. If you don't have direct access to them, you can watch them on video. If you are able to speak with them, ask them any questions that occur to you about how they know to do what they are doing and how they know when to do it.

3. When you feel like you have a real sense of what they do and how they do it, take some time to relax. Close your eyes and imagine yourself in a comfortable movie theater. You are about to watch a movie of your model of excellence, doing what it is they do so well.

4. After you've watched the movie through a few times, step into the image on the screen so you're seeing through their eyes, hearing through their ears, and feeling what they feel in their body.

   If for any reason that is uncomfortable for you, imagine yourself on screen next to them, shadowing their every move in perfect sync. Then step into your onscreen self, seeing through your eyes, hearing through your ears, and feeling what it feels like to do these new behaviors.

5. After you have repeated this process as many times as you like, step back out of the movie and return to the present moment, fully awake and alert.

Because the mind cannot easily tell the difference between a real experience and a vividly imagined one, you will be surprised at how effective you are when you begin to practice your new skill in the real world!

In the next chapter, I will be sharing some of the secrets of the world's fastest readers. Before long, you will be able to input written information in a fraction of the time you currently take and retain even more of that information than you probably do now. Until then, enjoy this quick review of everything in this chapter . . .

THE WHOLE CHAPTER IN ONE PAGE

- There are three levels of learning—gathering information, gaining a deeper understanding, and real-world application. Each level of learning is best accomplished by utilizing a particular learning strategy.

- To be able to gather and repeat information in an exam context, apply the memory strategies from Chapter 8.

- To gain a deeper understanding of the material you are learning, utilize chunking. You can chunk a difficult subject down into easy-to-learn, bite-size "chunks"; you can also take something that has a lot of separate parts and "chunk up" to a core idea or phrase.

- Mind mapping is a simple but effective way to combine chunking with whole brain learning by creating a visual representation of a topic or subject. It is useful as a way of gaining a deeper understanding of any topic, either for review or to prepare for a presentation or exam.

- To be able to quickly apply what you are learning in the real world, find an expert and use the modeling technique to quickly integrate their skills into your muscle memory.

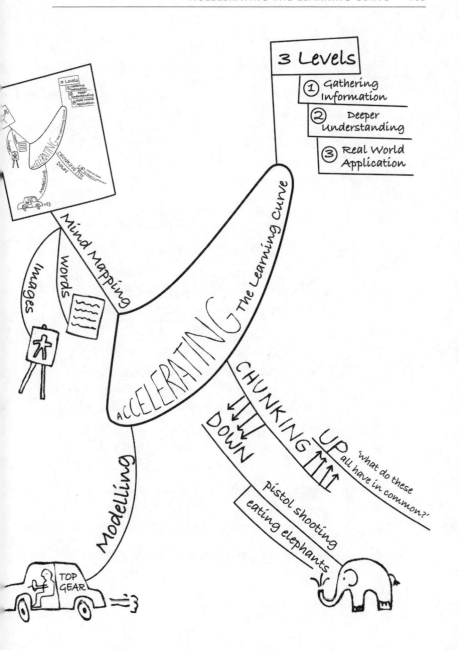

GET INTO THE ZONE!

Before you begin to read this chapter, check in to see if you are in your learning zone. If not, follow the steps below:

1. Take three slow and gentle breaths. Allow your body to relax and feel good.

2. Squeeze your thumb and middle finger together, firing off your "natural learning" anchor until you can begin to feel yourself going into a relaxed state of absorbed fascination.

3. Now, imagine what you would look like if you were just a little bit smarter than you are right now. How would you sit? What kind of expression would you have on your face? How would that smarter you show up in the world? How would they smile and interact with other people?

4. Step into that smarter you so that you're seeing what they see, hearing what they hear, and feeling the way they feel.

5. Set your concentration slider to the perfect blend of passive and active attention.

When you are ready, begin . . .

CHAPTER 7

•

Read for Speed

A Startling Experiment

Because I struggled with dyslexia growing up, reading was always a bit of a chore. So when I was filming a documentary for the British television network ITV and had the opportunity to sit down with Paul Scheele, creator of "PhotoReading," I jumped at the chance. PhotoReading is a revolutionary technique that suggests you can attain reading speeds of up to 65,000 words per minute—that's more than 250 times the speed of your average reader. While these claims were controversial, even at the time, I was keen to put them to the test.

The idea behind PhotoReading is that the limit on our reading speed is not taking in information, which can happen in the blink of an eye, but in consciously processing that information—that is, trying to make sense of what we read as we are reading it. In PhotoReading, people learn to use more of their minds by deliberately bypassing the conscious processing stage and allowing the words to go directly into the unconscious. Then, through a process of systematic training, they learn a variety of ways to "activate" that information and bring it back up into consciousness.

For the show, my producers wanted me to put this system to the test. So we went to Cray Research, a giant computer facility like something out of a James Bond movie. I was placed in front of one of their supercomputers and asked to look at a "Magic Eye" image, so that my eyes would be defocused and the words flashed up on the screen would bypass my conscious mind. Five minutes of barely visible flashing words later, I felt a bit dizzy and had to stop.

While I had no conscious idea of what I had seen, an hour later I was given a test on the material I had "studied." To my amazement, I got 76 percent of the answers correct—a full six points higher than the average comprehension score of someone reading at the standard rate of 250 words per minute.

Of course, reading in this way is not really practical—for starters, most of us don't have access to a supercomputer on a daily basis! But it opened my eyes to what was really possible.

Your Amazing Brain

Take a look at the following paragraph:

47 F1R57 Y0U M19H7 H4V3 7H0U9H7 Y0U 60ULDN'7 R34D 7H15, 8U7 8Y N0W Y0U KN0W Y0U 64N. 7H3 HUM4N M1ND 64N D0 3X7R40RD1N4RY 7H1N95. 17 15 4M421N9 4ND 50 4R3 Y0U!

You can make sense of it because your mind has a natural ability to pick out relevant patterns from huge quantities of data. In fact, it turns out that as with many things in life, 80 percent of the meaning in what you read is contained in only 20 percent of the words. By trying to read slowly and carefully and give each word equal weight, you actually limit the mind's natural ability to pull meaning from what it reads.

In addition, our brain is designed to "fill in the blanks" in our field of vision to allow us to see a more or less continuous image. This is why movies look like movies and not "moving pictures," which is a more accurate description. By flashing pictures up on a screen at a rate of at least 24 frames per second, filmmakers know that the human eye will fill in the blanks to create the illusion of continuous movement.

Until I had my experience with ultrafast reading on the computer, I thought it was important to consciously understand every word as I read it or else I wouldn't understand what came afterwards. But as we've already seen, our brains have the capacity to process information outside of the logical, sequential patterns of the left brain. And it's often only once we have the "big picture" of an article or book that we can really make sense of the details.

One way to understand why reading faster often actually increases comprehension is that our minds are designed to detect patterns, something that is virtually impossible when we slow down our visual input. Remember the stick figures kids would draw in the corner of schoolbooks like a sort of homemade cartoon movie? You would flip the pages of the book and the stick figure would come to life. Now imagine that you were only allowed to flip the pages at the rate of one per minute. All you would ever see was the individual drawings. The real "meaning" would be lost.

The same is true when we read. We actually need to go faster than we are initially comfortable with in order to enable our brains to make better sense of the material we are reading.

Finding Your Four Gears

I will now teach you four different ways to read and absorb written materials, from the slowest to the fastest. You will find that each type of reading lends itself to different types of material and to the specific goals behind your reading. I often mix and match styles, depending on my reading goals.

First Gear: Reading for Enjoyment

When the goal of your reading is simply to enjoy the experience, I encourage you to throw everything you're about to learn out of the window and simply allow yourself to read at what feels like a normal, comfortable pace. In fact, sometimes I slow down even more than usual when I'm reading for enjoyment, really taking the time to experience what I'm reading unfold like a rich, multisensory movie in my mind.

Second Gear: Accelerated Reading

Accelerated reading is simply a way to speed up your normal reading speed by training your brain to take in more words at a time more quickly than you are used to doing. Whereas most of us have learned to read one word at a time, accelerated readers can take in three to seven words per fixation.

To accelerate your reading, simply practice moving your hand along the lines on the page, following it with your eyes as you go. When your eyes become used to following your hand, you can just speed up your hand and your reading speed will increase along with it.

This one trick can increase your reading speed three to four times with no loss (and often some increase) in comprehension. That means you can read three books in the time it used to take you to read one, or devour research material for school or work in one third of the time it used to take you!

CALL TO ACTION

Test your reading speed

1. *Set an egg timer or countdown timer on your watch or phone to one minute.*

2. *Go to page 20 and begin reading at your normal speed. Stop and mark your place when your time is up.*

3. *Count up the number of lines of text you've just read. For the purposes of this test, you can assume that each line has an average of ten words in it.*

4. *To calculate your approximate reading speed, multiply the number of lines you read times by ten. Your answer will be the number of words per minute you currently read.*

    Example: *You read 23 lines of text. 23 x 10 = 230, so your current reading speed is approximately 230 words per minute.*

5. *Return to this test after you have spent some time practicing the techniques in this chapter and notice how your reading speed has increased!*

Third Gear: Super Read and Dip

To understand the idea behind "Super Reading," Paul Scheele uses the analogy of Superman coming to Earth for the first time:

> *From an aerial distance of one hundred thousand miles, you see the Earth as a swirling blue ball. You set a flight path straight toward the planet. From ten thousand miles away you can start to make out the outlines of continents. You also notice how much of the planet is covered by water. Zooming in closer, you notice the variegated land surfaces: deserts, rain forests, prairies, and mountains.*
>
> *Suddenly, you are attracted to a lush, green island with a sandy beach and a magnificent ocean view. You touch down, spend a short time exploring the terrain, and take a quick dip in the water. Satisfied, you take to the skies again, searching for another place to land.*

In the same way, when you "Super Read," you are flying over the text, allowing yourself to be drawn by whatever interests you and then resuming your overview until the next thing that draws you in.

The other addition to your reading strategy while in third gear is to take the time to get clear about your goal for what it is you are about to read. Since in Super Reading you are no longer trying to read every single word or understand every single sentence, setting a clear intention in this way will help your unconscious mind to guide you towards the exact sections of the book or article that will be most relevant to the goal you have in mind. Here's all you need to do:

SUPER READ AND DIP

Read the technique all the way through before you start.

1. Think about your goal for reading this book or article. Is it to be able to learn key facts to prepare for an exam, to gain deeper understanding and insight into a subject that interests you, or is it part of the process of learning a new skill?

2. Place your hand at the top of the page and move it straight down the middle, following your hand with your eyes. Your goal is to focus directly enough to recognize as many words as you can without actively trying to understand what you are reading as you read it.

3. When your attention is drawn to a particular section of the text, slow down enough to read through it in detail, then go back to Super Reading the rest of the text until you find the next section you are drawn to.

Remember, in Super Reading you are no longer trying to understand what you read as you read it—but because you are still going slowly enough to consciously recognize the words, you will be drawn easily into the sections that are most relevant to fulfilling your reading goals.

Fourth Gear: PhotoReading

Imagine you are going on a hike. Before you begin, you climb to the top of a nearby hill and look out over the beautiful landscape you will be hiking through. As you scan the landscape, you get a sense of the different types of terrain and a feel for the nature of what it is you are looking at. While you are not deliberately trying to notice detail, certain things will jump out at you.

In the same way, PhotoReading is an excellent way to get a snapshot or an overview of a book or article in a very short space of time. Whereas with traditional reading you read one word at a time, PhotoReading allows you to read one or two pages at a time. When you are done you might not have a precise knowledge of where every twig and branch is placed, but you have a clear sense of the overall terrain.

Our eyes contain over 260 million light receptors, only 15 percent of which are designed to take in what we are focused on directly, known as our "foveal vision." Whatever we see in our foveal vision is channeled through our conscious mind, which is the way you have been reading up until this point. But the other

85 percent of our visual field, called "peripheral vision," is designed to take in information *outside* of our conscious awareness.

A fun way to experience the kind of soft, easy focus that activates your peripheral vision is to point your index fingers at each other and bring them closer together until you can see the "blip finger" that appears in between them.

Once you can do that consistently, apply the same soft focus to the pages of this book. Keep your eyes relaxed and focus on a point in the distance slightly above the top of this book. In your peripheral vision, you will begin to notice a "blip page" appear—like a smaller rounded page between the two actual pages. Move your eyes slightly downwards until you can be looking directly at the book but still seeing the "blip page" in the center.

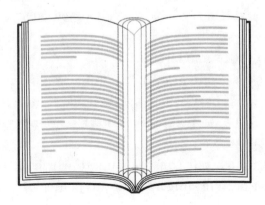

By softening your focus and expanding your visual field as you read, you will take in substantially more information and "download" it directly into your unconscious. Once the download is complete, you can then "activate" the information by asking yourself questions about the material or making a mind map.

An Important Note:

PhotoReading is designed to deliberately bypass your conscious mind. This means that at first you may feel that you are wasting your time, as none of the information you are reading is going in consciously and you are not even consciously seeing the words on the page while you read. If you persist with your practice, over time you will begin to notice yourself "just knowing" things that were contained in the books you PhotoRead as if they floated up into your mind from your unconscious. You will also be left with a clear sense of what each book is about and even which sections of the book are worth revisiting later in more depth.

HOW TO PHOTOREAD

Read the technique all the way through before you start.

1. Think about your goal for reading this book or article. Is it to be able to learn key facts to prepare for an exam, to gain deeper understanding and insight into a subject that interests you, or is it part of the process of learning a new skill?

2. With your goal clearly in mind, skim through the book to get a sense of its structure. Notice what's in the table of contents, chapter headings, and anything that's broken out into separate sec- tions—the "terrain" of the book. It's a bit like preparing for a slalom ski race—before skiing down the mountain, you'd look to see where the flags were so you could get a sense of the route ahead of you.

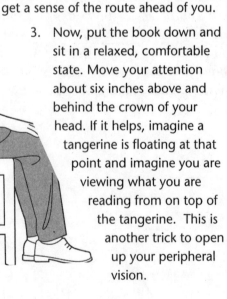

3. Now, put the book down and sit in a relaxed, comfortable state. Move your attention about six inches above and behind the crown of your head. If it helps, imagine a tangerine is floating at that point and imagine you are viewing what you are reading from on top of the tangerine. This is another trick to open up your peripheral vision.

4. With your goal in mind and your attention above and behind the back of your head, look down at the book. Allow your visual field to expand and soften until you can see the "blip page," or at the very least the space around the four edges of the book.

5. Now, simply turn the pages one at a time at a rate of about a page every two seconds. You are not trying to read the words, but simply letting the information imprint itself directly into your unconscious mind.

6. When you finish the book, put it down and close your eyes. Allow the information a bit of time to settle before going back to it, like you would take time to allow a good meal to digest.

7. At this point you can either PhotoRead another book on the subject you are studying or "downshift" into a lower gear to go deeper into the detail of the information.

There are books, home study courses, and even live events where you can learn PhotoReading in much more depth from certified trainers and teachers, but you don't have to wait until you've done a course to begin using the technique. I recommend always PhotoReading a book before you actually begin to read it in the lower three gears.

This is the essence of what is called "layered reading." By first previewing the material, then overviewing it and then going back through it in more and more depth until you are essentially reviewing it, you will learn much more than you would by slowly reading through it one time.

Each time you go back through the material it becomes more familiar to you, and you will find you get much more out of it than if you just picked up the book and began to read it "cold." Because of the much faster speeds at which you will be reading in the higher gears, you can often go through the material three to five times in less time than it would take to read it once in the old-fashioned way.

CALL TO ACTION

Use the reading gears

Go back to the beginning of the book and practice using each of the "reading gears": PhotoRead it from beginning to end, then Super Read and Dip, and finally go back and Accelerated Read it from the beginning back to this point. You'll be amazed at how much more you get out of it each time you do!

As with everything you are learning throughout this book, your results over time will be a product of the state you are in as you read, the strategies you are using, and the amount and quality of practice time you put in. The more you practice, the easier and more effective your reading skills will become.

In the next chapter, we will be looking at the secrets of getting the most from your memory. Until then, enjoy this brief review of the key ideas, strategies, and concepts in this chapter . . .

THE WHOLE CHAPTER IN ONE PAGE

- Using your whole brain allows you to read faster.

- You can read in at least four different gears—for pleasure, accelerated, Super Read and Dip, and PhotoRead.

- For most reading, you will use your foveal vision. For PhotoReading, you will activate and use your peripheral vision.

- Layered reading allows you to get much more out of material than one-off reading.

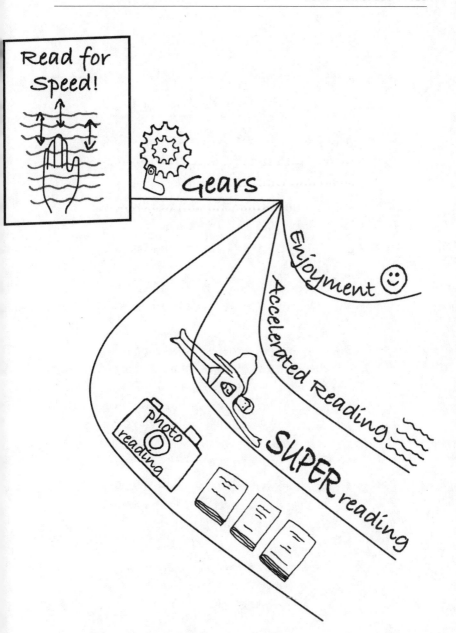

GET INTO THE ZONE!

Before you begin to read this chapter, check in to see if you are in your learning zone. If not, follow the steps below:

1. Take three slow and gentle breaths. Allow your body to relax and feel good.

2. Squeeze your thumb and middle finger together, firing off your "natural learning" anchor until you can begin to feel yourself going into a relaxed state of absorbed fascination.

3. Now, imagine what you would look like if you were just a little bit smarter than you are right now. How would you sit? What kind of expression would you have on your face? How would that smarter you show up in the world? How would they smile and interact with other people?

4. Step into that smarter you so that you're seeing what they see, hearing what they hear, and feeling the way they feel.

5. Set your concentration slider to the perfect blend of passive and active attention.

When you are ready, begin . . .

CHAPTER 8

•

The Secrets
of a
Supercharged
Memory

A Memorable Party Trick

One of my favorite party tricks is to ask people to come up with a list of 10 to 20 random things. In three minutes or less, I will then memorize them in sequence without writing them down and repeat them back both forwards and backwards.

The really good part of the trick comes next—I offer to teach anyone at the party how to do exactly the same thing. Within just a few minutes, they too are able to repeat the same trick, albeit with a slightly shorter list to start off with.

By the end of this chapter, you too will be able to perform this memory trick, but better still you will know the secret of remembering long lists of facts or vocabulary words for an examination. The reason I can teach you to do this so quickly is because having a supercharged memory, like everything else you have been learning in this book, is simply a function of being in a resourceful state, using an effective strategy and practicing until it becomes second nature. Once you know the strategy, the only "trick" is to practice.

The other thing that will help you is to have a deeper understanding of how memory actually works.

The Nature of Memory

I have assisted the police on several occasions in relation to some interesting cases. With a bit of time and care, it is often possible to help a witness recall information that they saw or heard but did not consciously remember. The process is to gently build on whatever small details the person does remember until a fuller representation of the incident comes back to life.

In one case a witness had been on the street where a hit and run took place but couldn't remember the license plate. I began by asking him what the weather was like on that day.

"Yeah, I remember the sun was shining," he said.

"And what do you remember about the street you were walking down?"

He then began to describe the street he had been on. I asked him to go into as much sensory detail as he could, and he told me about the feeling of the pavement beneath his feet, the smell in the air, what sounds he was hearing, and eventually more and more details of what he could see. By the time we were done, he had provided a whole series of details about the scene that proved helpful to the investigation, including the complete license plate number of the car.

The reason this technique, known as "cognitive interview," works has to do with the nature of memory:

Everything that ever happens to us is recorded and stored as a multisensory recording in the unconscious mind.

The old theory about memory was that our past experiences and information are all sort of stored away in our brain in a series of filing cabinets, with short-term memories at the front and older memories in long-term storage at the back. But long-term memory works more like a spider's web, where one strand of memory connects with the next until the entire web of memory is held together.

So just asking somebody to remember something prompts their brain to begin the process of tracing its way along the strands of the web. The more sensory detail they are asked to recall, the stronger each individual strand becomes. Soon, the entire web (memory) becomes more visible. This process takes time, so it's important not to be in a rush and to really allow time for the full memory to come back into consciousness.

Another analogy for long-term memory is a different type of web—the World Wide Web most of us use every single day. This web is made up of a series of interlinked pages. When we begin researching a topic on one page, that then links us to several others, and if we care enough to really learn we can eventually find the information we are looking for.

In this sense, your memory works like a muscle—the more you use it, the stronger it gets. Here is an excellent exercise you can practice daily to improve your memory for life. It will form a part of the daily mind workout you will be learning in Chapter 14.

TIME TO REMEMBER

Read the technique all the way through before you start.

1. Think of a happy memory from your past. It can be recent or from your childhood—all that matters is that it is something you are happy to remember now.

2. Step back into the memory so that you're seeing it through your own eyes, as if you're back there now. Notice whether the first thing you notice about the memory is an image, a sound, a smell, a taste, or a feeling. Whatever it is, begin by describing that memory aloud, focusing on whichever sense is the most vivid for you.

3. After a minute or so, continue to explore your memory using another sense—sight, sound, taste, smell, or touch. When you have a vivid representation of it, move on to the next sense.

    Example: *When I think about working at Radio Caroline, I can see the beautiful Icelandic trawler with a magnificent mast, the sun shining on the dark blue gray waves of the Atlantic Ocean. I can see the studio with the old rotary-style controls and the wall of records behind it. I can hear the sound of "Drive" by the Cars playing over the ship's speakers, and the Radio Caroline bell at the top of each hour. I can feel the slight rocking motion of the boat, the mist of the sea air on my face, and the hard, cold metal surface of the boat through my sneakers. The smell of fresh sea air was everywhere, along with the faint stench of diesel fuel burning on the lower decks.*

The Power of Association

The actor Peter Bowles came to see me a few years back for assistance in learning a part. He was due to appear in a Sir Peter Hall production of a Molière play in a part that required him to recite nearly 20 minutes' worth of rhyming couplets. He was struggling to remember his words, and it became clear almost immediately that it was because he was attempting to use the wrong strategy.

In preparing for film and television roles, the smaller number of lines allowed him to learn by rote, through hours of simple repetition. But the sheer number and complexity of lines in the play meant that strategy would never work, at least not without a herculean amount of time and effort on his part.

And the strategy he normally used to learn a play involved him building strong associations between the environment and story of the play and the lines he was trying to remember. Each line had an associated action and was part of the larger story being told. So if he walks into a room, there is a line associated with that action. When he sits down, that reminds him of his next line, and then when someone sits down next to him, that triggers another line, all within the context of the overall plot.

But because in this instance there was little or no action to help him link the lines together, I asked him to imagine the actual imagery behind the lines as if it was happening in real time. When he had to talk about a "king arriving from a far-off land," in his mind's eye he would imagine a king actually arriving with a huge retinue, using big, bold multisensory imagery that would stick in his mind. Now, instead of just trying to remember the words in isolation, he was using them to recall specific images and tell a story.

This is what nearly all memory experts do—they use the power of association to connect seemingly unconnected things and then exaggerate that imagery to make the associations more memorable.

There are essentially five keys to creating memorable associations—exaggeration, movement, sexual imagery, bizarre humor, and synesthesia. Synesthesia is a naturally occurring phenomenon where we experience a multisensory representation of something. Each time throughout this book that I've asked you to "see what you saw, hear what you heard, and feel how good you felt," I've been utilizing synesthesia to help you create a more memorable experience.

To experience the power of association for yourself, read the following section slowly, taking the time to vividly imagine each scene before moving forward:

You are riding naked on the back of a purple elephant in the front room of your home. The smell is horrible, so you dismount from the elephant and the two of you step into the shower and lather each other up.

To your dismay, you can hear Darth Vader outside the shower, breathing heavily. When you poke your head out from the curtain to ask him to be quiet, you notice that he is seated at a giant yellow piano, getting ready to play. Instead of normal hands, he has ten wiggly haddock where his fingers ought to be.

Now let me ask you a few questions—do your best not to look back at the preceding paragraph while you are answering them . . .

- *What kind of animal were you riding?*
- *What did you do after dismounting?*
- *Who was outside breathing heavily?*
- *Where were they sitting?*
- *What did they have instead of fingers?*

Chances are you were able to answer all of those questions without much difficulty. But if I had asked you to memorize a random list of words consisting of "elephant," "shower," "Darth Vader," "piano," and "haddock," you would have struggled.

Here's a practical application of the power of association you can use to remember anyone's name in just a few moments . . .

WHAT'S IN A NAME?

There are only two things you need to do to remember a name:

1. Do something unusual to alert your brain to pay extra attention.

2. Create a vivid, memorable association between the person's face and their name using exaggeration, movement, sexual imagery, bizarre humor, and synesthesia.

Here is my own favorite way of doing that— you may come up with your own preferred ways of doing it as you practice.

- When I first meet someone, I repeat their name aloud several times. (The journalist David Frost reputedly repeats a person's name 20 times when he first meets them.) This alerts my brain to pay extra attention to something that normally happens completely unconsciously.

- If the person has the same name as someone I know very well, I use bizarre imagery to visualize them with two heads—their own, and that of the person I already know with the same name.

- If they have a name I am less familiar with, I imagine that it is written in lights on a theater marquee above a giant photograph of their face.

How to Remember Lists of Pretty Much Anything

The strategy I promised to share with you at the beginning of this chapter is said to have originally been developed in the 5th century B.C. A Greek poet named Sionides of Ceos found that he could remember every one of the ill-fated guests at a banquet that had been brought to a premature close when the roof of the building collapsed on top of them. He noticed that, by remembering the layout of the room itself, he could automatically recall who had been sitting where.

He then developed a technique that is used by memory experts to this day—what memory experts call the "memory palace." Of course, you don't need to use an actual palace. By vividly imagining the layout of any physical location, like your home or office or even the route to work or the setting of your favorite TV show, you then have an easy way to associate random lists of names, dates, or pretty much anything to something you are already intimately familiar with.

To begin constructing your very own memory palace, imagine you are giving an important guest a tour of your home. What is the first room you show them? The next? The next? For now, make sure you have at least five locations marked out in the order you would visit them. Your "palace" doesn't actually have to have five different rooms—you can simply use different parts of one room as separate locations. For example, if you were using your kitchen, you might choose the refrigerator, the stove, the countertops, the window, and the doorway as your first five locations.

When you have your five rooms or locations ready, we are going to put this into practice. Here is a new list of five random items:

Camera	Tent	Trombone	Harry Potter	Birthday Cake

I want you to create an associational link between each item and the first five locations in your memory palace. Remember to place just one item in each location, and to make those associations exaggerated, moving, sexual, bizarrely humorous, and multisensory.

When you think you've got them, write them down. (If that seems too easy, recall the list in reverse order by beginning in the last location and going back towards the beginning . . .)

The more you practice this strategy, the faster and more consistently you will be able to use it. Of course, when you want or need to remember longer lists, you simply need to first create a larger memory palace.

Memory champions use this technique to remember everything from to-do lists to entire dictionaries—the only limitation on how much you can remember is the size and number of the memory palaces you create. As well as your home and office, you can use the route you take to work, a public park, or indeed any space with which you are or can become intimately familiar.

CALL TO ACTION

Build your "palace"

Take a bit of time right now to build a palace with at least 25 separate locations in it. Imagine yourself walking around it, being sure to always move from location to location in the same sequence. The more thoroughly you create your memory palace now, the more useful it will be to you in the future!

Once you have created your first memory palace, you will be able to put it into practice for everything from remembering shopping lists to preparing for exams. I cannot stress often enough that the only obstacle to success in creating a supercharged memory is your willingness and determination to practice!

CALL TO ACTION

Learn people's names

Deliberately meet five new people today and learn their names. Choose people you are liable to bump into again, from the person behind the counter at your favorite coffee shop to a fellow passenger on your journey into work. Take the time to repeat their names aloud to alert your brain to pay extra attention, and then create a vivid, memorable association to "lock in" the memory so it will easily come to mind the next time you see them.

An Important Caveat

It's important to realize that no matter how much you practice, nobody's memory is infallible. In fact, one of the world's leading memory experts told me that he was once so engrossed in preparing for a memory test he forgot to pick his mother up from the airport!

Rather than judge your memory against a standard of perfection, notice where your use of these techniques causes it to improve. Over time, these small improvements can make a huge difference.

In the next chapter, I'll be revealing some basic strategies for math and spelling that will either serve as a gentle review or form the basis of a whole new understanding of what's possible. Before then, take a few moments now to review the key points from this chapter . . .

THE WHOLE CHAPTER IN ONE PAGE

- Everything you see, hear, and feel is permanently stored in your memory. The only question is access.

- In order to access memories more easily, it is important to remember that memory is not a filing system, but an associative trigger system.

- You can strengthen your memory through practice. In particular, practice remembering things using one sensory system at a time.

- You can make anything more memorable by using imagery that is exaggerated, moving, sexual, bizarrely humorous, and multisensory.

- Use repetition and association to remember names.

- Use a "memory palace" to remember lists of pretty much anything.

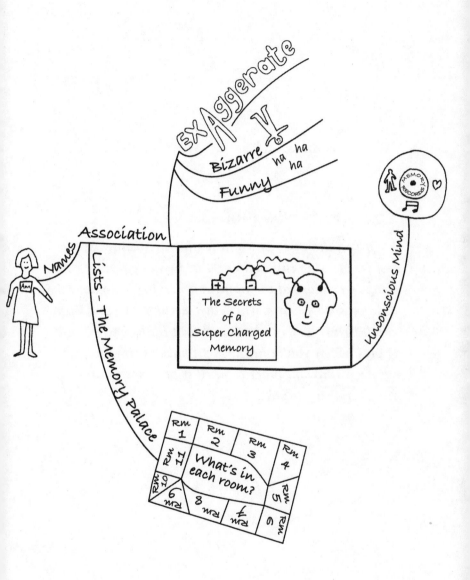

A QUICK NOTE FROM PAUL:

If you are already a math whiz or spelling genius, feel free to skip this chapter. But if you're feeling your palms go sweaty at the thought of having to do a math quiz or spell a word while the pictures in your head go all fuzzy, read on—you will find that as with most things, when you're in the right state, using the right strategy, and you practice until it becomes second nature, anything is possible!

CHAPTER 9

•

Math Myths and Spelling Secrets

The Millionaire and the Schoolboy

When I was in school, I remember one particular story that caught my attention. It was about a millionaire who spotted an ingenious business idea that a schoolboy came up with and offered to buy it for the princely sum of $1,000. The schoolboy knew the businessman would be able to turn his idea into millions, so he made him a different offer: he would sell him the rights to his idea for a penny, providing the millionaire would double his money for 30 days—a penny on day one, two pennies on day two, four pennies on day three, and so on.

The millionaire chuckled to himself at the schoolboy's naiveté, but reassured himself that everyone needs to learn about the ways of the world and quickly agreed to the bargain. To his dismay, one month later, he discovered he had paid the boy over $10 million!

I couldn't believe it, but our teacher showed us the math:

DAY 1 $0.01	DAY 2 $0.02	DAY 3 $0.04	DAY 4 $0.08	DAY 5 $0.16	DAY 6 $0.32
DAY 7 $0.64	DAY 8 $1.28	DAY 9 $2.56	DAY 10 $5.12	DAY 11 $10.24	DAY 12 $20.48
DAY 13 $40.96	DAY 14 $81.92	DAY 15 $163.84	DAY 16 $327.68	DAY 17 $655.36	DAY 18 $1,310.72
DAY 19 $2,621.44	DAY 20 $5,242.88	DAY 21 $10,485.76	DAY 22 $20,971.52	DAY 23 $41,943.04	DAY 24 $83,886.08
DAY 25 $167,772.16	DAY 26 $335,544.32	DAY 27 $671,088.64	DAY 28 **$1,342,177.28**	DAY 29 $2,684,354.56	DAY 30 $5,368,709.12

For a grand total of $10,737,418.23!

While I won't pretend that this story turned me into a mathematical genius—I got mediocre grades in math—it did make me recognize that in the right context, math could be interesting and even a little bit fun. What I still had to overcome was my own discomfort with numbers.

What's so Scary about Numbers?

Many people I meet are convinced that they are no good at numbers and never can be. Some have such bad associations with math that it borders on a phobia. These negative associations seem to have been installed in people at school and reinforced by their teachers and peers until they not only believe they can't do math, they actually go into mental lockdown at the very thought of having to try. Which makes sense if you think about standing at the blackboard as a young child and being laughed at when you can't solve a problem, or having all your mistakes pointed out in bright red pen every time you did a page of homework, or took a quiz or exam.

Even those people who don't think about math as scary are often put off learning more by some of the odd hypnotic suggestions that have become a part of our cultural mythology, including:

- **"You're either good at numbers or good at words. Nobody but a total nerd is good at both!"**

- **"Girls aren't good at math—it's just not how their brains work."**

- **"What's the point in learning math? That's what calculators are for!"**

Now, if you already love math, you can skip this next exercise, but if you have any hesitation at all about learning more, it's worthwhile revisiting the Instant Block Remover (aka Havening) from Chapter 3 to clear away any residual fears about math you may be harboring. Once we've eliminated any blocks you may have been holding on to, I'll share some simple strategies to master the basics . . .

TAKING THE STRESS OUT OF MATH

Read the technique all the way through before you start.

1.   What are some of the "math myths" you have been carrying with you since school? Allow your mind to wander back and remember all the worst struggles you have had with math over the years, or imagine you are about to be asked to solve a math problem. Notice how much stress or discomfort you are feeling on a scale of 1 to 10.

2.   Now clear your mind, or just think about something nice.

3.   Next, use both hands to tap on both your collarbones.

4.   While you continue tapping on both your collarbones, look straight ahead, keep your head still, and close and open your eyes.

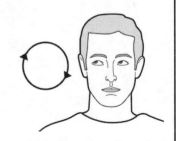

5.   Continue tapping and, keeping your head still, look down to the left then down to the right.

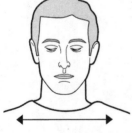

6.   Continue tapping, keeping your head still, and move your eyes in a full circle clockwise and then counterclockwise.

7. Now cross your arms, place your hands on the tops of your shoulders, and close your eyes.

8. Now stroke your hands down the sides of your arms from your shoulders to your elbows, down and up, again and again.

9. As you carry on stroking the sides of your arms, imagine you are walking down a flight of stairs and count out loud from 1 to 20 with each step you take.

10. When you reach 20, hum "Happy Birthday."

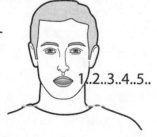

11. Now, let your arms drop and relax them, and open your eyes and look up in front of and above you.

12. Move your eyes slowly from left to right and back three times.

13. Close your eyes and stroke the sides of your arms again five times.

14. Now open your eyes and think about learning some new math skills. On your scale from 1 to 10, what number is the feeling now?

If it is down to a 3 or less, go on with the rest of the chapter. If you think that the stressful feeling is not yet reduced enough, just repeat the sequence until it is reduced as far as you want.

Strategies for Success

Over the years, I have come to believe that everyone is capable of not only learning math, but also enjoying the process. While not all math is relevant to all professions, there aren't many jobs out there that don't require at least the basics. In this sense, not having at least a basic understanding of numbers is almost as limiting as not being able to read.

As with everything else we have been learning throughout this book, there are only three variables that will determine your level of performance:

1. **The state you are in.**

2. **The strategy you are using.**

3. **The amount and quality of practice you put in.**

So sit back, relax, and let me share three simple strategies to get you started . . .

Strategy number one: Left to right

I don't know about you, but I was taught to read from left to right but to do basic calculations from right to left. Yet when you think about it, the most important numbers are on the left. If you were being paid $50.37 for a job, would you rather they made the mistake with the $50 or with the 37 cents?

Take this simple problem, for example:

$$38$$
$$+ 24$$
$$\overline{}$$

In school, I was taught to first add the ones, then the tens, and so on from right to left. But let's do it the other way . . .

$$3(0) + 2(0) = 50$$
$$8 + 4 = 12$$

$$50 + 12 = 62$$

Or this one, with three numbers in each column:

$$836$$
$$+ 781$$
$$\overline{}$$

Going from left to right, we start with the hundreds column:

$$8(00) + 7(00) = 1500$$
$$3(0) + 8(0) = 110$$
$$6 + 1 = 7$$

For a final answer of 1617.

Try these for yourself. You'll find the answers on page 160. As with anything, the more you practice, the easier it gets!

12	38	71	95	129
+ 15	+ 23	+ 45	+ 87	+ 81
322	533	8910	704	7299
+ 149	+ 291	+ 3186	652	546
			+ 117	+ 89

Strategy number two: Multiplication from memory

Multiplication is really just a shortcut for addition. For example, 5x5 is just a simpler way of adding 5+5+5+5+5. Because we're adding 5 five times, we say 5x5.

It is also one of the few things in life that is learned best by rote—that is, by simply drilling the basic times tables again and again until you know all the pairings from 1x1 to 12x12 by heart.

While that may take a little time, once you've done it you'll never struggle with a multiplication (or division!) problem ever again . . .

X	1	2	3	4	5	6	7	8	9	10	11	12
1	1	2	3	4	5	6	7	8	9	10	11	12
2	2	4	6	8	10	12	14	16	18	20	22	24
3	3	6	9	12	15	18	21	24	27	30	33	36
4	4	8	12	16	20	24	28	32	36	40	44	48
5	5	10	15	20	25	30	35	40	45	50	55	60
6	6	12	18	24	30	36	42	48	54	60	66	72
7	7	14	21	28	35	42	49	56	63	70	77	84
8	8	16	24	32	40	48	56	64	72	80	88	96
9	9	18	27	36	45	54	63	72	81	90	99	108
10	10	20	30	40	50	60	70	80	90	100	110	120
11	11	22	33	44	55	66	77	88	99	110	121	132
12	12	24	36	48	60	72	84	96	108	120	132	144

As with most things, our brain learns quickly more easily than it can learn slowly. The faster you practice, the quicker you'll learn. Use a stopwatch and time yourself doing the whole table from the 12s down to the 1s like this:

12, 24, 36, 48, 60, 72, 84, 96, 108, 120, 132, 144
11, 22, 33, 44, 55, 66, 77, 88, 99, 110, 121, 132
10, 20, 30, 40, 50, 60, 70, 80, 90, 100, 110, 120

and so on all the way down to . . .

1, 2, 3, 4, 5, 6, 7, 8, 9, 10, 11, 12

Your first few times may take you a few minutes, but if you practice, before long you'll be able to do the whole thing in 90 seconds or less!

Once you've got your multiplication tables from 1 to 12 locked into your unconscious memory so they're there whenever you need them, you can multiply numbers of any size by simply going one column at a time.

For example, before I understood how it worked, a problem like this would have had me closing my math book determined to buy a really good calculator and never try to solve a math problem again:

$$523$$
$$\times 8$$

But now that I realize I will never have to multiply any two numbers that aren't in my basic times tables, I can break it down like this, once again using my left-to-right strategy:

$$
\begin{aligned}
5(00) \times 8 &= 40(00) \\
2(0) \times 8 &= 16(0) \\
3 \times 8 &= 24 \\
4000 + 160 + 24 &= 4184
\end{aligned}
$$

If this feels too advanced for you, slow things down and go back to the basics. Stick with learning your times tables until you can do it in under a minute, then come back to the rest. And if you're feeling overwhelmed, you can go back and repeat the "Taking the stress out of math" technique from earlier in the chapter.

Strategy number three: Estimate for success

In the real world, "close enough" is nearly always close enough. I have bookkeepers and accountants who do my accounts and can make sure all the t's are crossed and all the i's are dotted, but for me, being able to estimate quickly and accurately allows me to do most of what I need to do.

Here is the only trick you need to quickly estimate anything from the figures for your business to almost any application of basic math:

> **Round the numbers up or down *before* the calculation to make things easier**

Since in estimation we're not concerned with getting the exact answer, we can round the numbers we're working with up or down to the nearest "simple" number to use in our calculation.

For example, if I've got payments due of $453.29, $193.74, and $28.06, I would round those off to $450, $200, and $30. Adding from left to right (remember that one?), I know I'm going to be spending about 6(00) + 8(0), or around $680.

You can do the same thing with multiplication:

$$52 \times 48 = ?$$

If I round 52 down to 50 and 48 up to 50, and then I multiply and add my zeroes afterwards, I get 5x5 = 25 plus two zeroes = 2500. (According to my calculator, the actual answer is 2496. In other words, we're only off by 4 and we were able to do the whole thing in our head!)

Spelling Secrets

Some people feel that numbers are easy because they always follow the same logical patterns, even though sometimes the patterns can get quite complex. The spelling of certain words, on the other hand, often seems like it was made up at random.

So when he wanted to find a reliable way of teaching anyone how to spell, Dr. Richard Bandler began by studying naturally gifted spellers. And he quickly noticed a dramatic difference between the strategy used by kids who were excellent spellers and those who struggled. The great spellers employed a primarily visual strategy—that is, they would actually see the word in their mind's eye as they spelled it. In contrast, the poor and average spellers would almost always try to sound out each word "phonetically."

To be a great speller yourself, use their strategies:

a. **Hear the word and/or say the word in your mind.**

b. **Make a picture in your head of the word spelled correctly, occasionally checking it against a picture of the same word spelled incorrectly.**

c. **Check to see which spelling "feels right."**

By using that same basic strategy—say the word, see it spelled right in your mind, and check it against a feeling—we now have a simple way of teaching ourselves to spell.

In order to use more of your mind and brain, you can write the words in different colors and sizes, particularly if there are any unusual or silent letters in the word.

For example:

BiGGEr
ChRYSaNTHEMuM
PHONETiCaLLy

If a word seems too long to learn in one go, you can also break your word picture down into smaller chunks:

BiG GEr
ChRYS aNTHE MuM
PHONE TiCaL Ly

Take some time now to go through the natural spelling strategy . . .

NATURAL SPELLING

Read the technique all the way through before you start.

1. Write down the word you want to learn. At the risk of stating the obvious, be sure to spell it correctly!

2. Move your eyes down to your right and think of something that feels familiar, comfortable, or "just right." (You can do this with your eyes open or closed.) When you are in touch with that feeling, open your eyes and look at the word.

3. Now, move your eyes up and to your left and picture the correct spelling in your mind's eye. (It may be helpful to actually hold the piece of paper slightly up and to your left so you can see it with your eyes in that position.)

4. Put the paper away and spell the word out loud by "reading" it in your mind. Now, check it against the paper. If you haven't spelled it right, simply repeat steps 2 to 4 until you have.

5. Now, look back up and to the left and spell the word BACKWARDS—that is, read it in your mind from right to left. This step ensures that the word is "locked" into your visual memory. Again, if you spell the word incorrectly, simply repeat the process from the beginning.

What's wonderful about this strategy is that once you have memorized a certain number of words in this way, your mind will begin to generalize the pattern—that is, your brain will begin to teach itself to spell ALL words this way, whether or not you have taken the time to write each new word out. At that point, you will not only have taught yourself to spell—you will have become a great speller!

The answers to the sums on page 152 are: 27, 61, 116, 182, 210, 471, 824, 12096, 1473, 7934

Time for a Break . . .

We've covered a lot in this chapter, so before you move forward to learn the ultimate formula for exam success, why not take a break and review the key ideas and mind map on the following pages?

THE WHOLE CHAPTER IN ONE PAGE

- If we fear numbers, it's because we were taught to fear them at school—usually by other people who grew up fearing numbers.

- It's easier to add from left to right than from right to left.

- Multiplication is just a shortcut for addition.

- Once you have memorized your times tables from 1 to 12, you can multiply any number in the world, no matter how large.

- Estimation is the key to real-world math—all you need to do is practice rounding up and rounding down to make the math as simple as possible.

- Spelling is easy if you do it visually, not by sounding words out.

- Once you can spell a word backwards, you will be able to spell it forever!

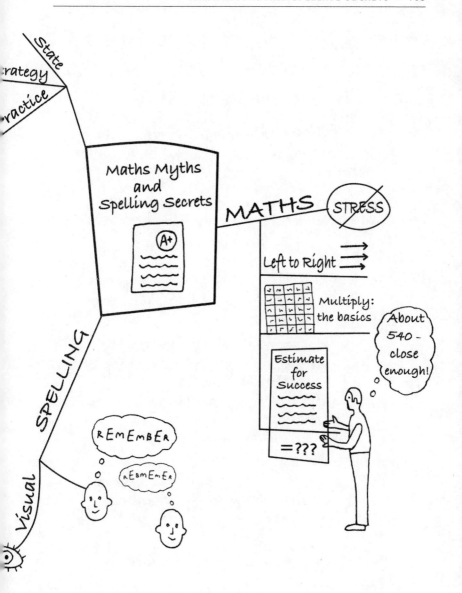

GET INTO THE ZONE!

Before you begin to read this chapter, check in to see if you are in your learning zone. If not, follow the steps below:

1. Take three slow and gentle breaths. Allow your body to relax and feel good.

2. Squeeze your thumb and middle finger together, firing off your "natural learning" anchor until you can begin to feel yourself going into a relaxed state of absorbed fascination.

3. Now, imagine what you would look like if you were just a little bit smarter than you are right now. How would you sit? What kind of expression would you have on your face? How would that smarter you show up in the world? How would they smile and interact with other people?

4. Step into that smarter you so that you're seeing what they see, hearing what they hear, and feeling the way they feel.

5. Set your concentration slider to the perfect blend of passive and active attention.

When you are ready, begin . . .

CHAPTER 10

•

The Ultimate Formula
for Exam Success

The Ultimate Formula for Exam Success

One of the definitions of the word "formula" is this:

A method, pattern, or rule for doing or producing something, often one proved to be successful.

When it comes to exam success, the formula is simple:

Exam success is ⅓ study, ⅓ state, and ⅓ strategy.

In other words, there are actually three keys to succeeding at exams—the effectiveness of your revision, the resourcefulness of your state, and the appropriateness of the strategy you use for the exam.

In this chapter, I will take you through all three steps and share some of the most powerful strategies I have discovered and put to the test for creating exam success. Unlike other chapters in this book, I am simply going to give you instructions to follow, step by step. You can always adapt these instructions to fit your particular situation . . .

STEP ONE OF THREE: STUDY FOR SUCCESS
Timing Is Everything

The "best" way to study is 100 percent a function of how much time you have in which to do it. To create your study schedule, simply divide the amount of material you need to study by the amount of time you have to study it in. The more time you have, the more relaxed a schedule you can create. The less time, the more focused you will need to be.

For example, if you have five exams coming up in five weeks' time, you could choose to study one subject a week or one subject a day for five weeks, e.g., math each Monday, history each Tuesday, geography each Wednesday, physics each Thursday, and French each Friday.

If you only have two weeks to go before your big history final and there are 14 chapters for you to revise, you can do one a day over the fortnight, or two a day the first week and then review them in the second week.

But even if you're reading this the night before the big exam, it's not too late!

Simply look over all your course materials, review your mind maps and notes, and listen to the "Exam Confidence" hypnotic trance before getting a good night's sleep. While this cannot and will not replicate the value of actually studying over time, it is dramatically more effective than an intense all-night "attack" on your materials.

Recent research has shown that the mind and body have their own pattern of rest or alertness with one predominant cycle called "the ultradian rhythm" that occurs approximately every 90 minutes. This is a part of your body's own natural stress-control mechanism, when it attempts to pull your focus away from the outside world as it takes five to fifteen minutes to relax and refresh its energy.

Unfortunately, many people ignore this message from their body, especially in the days and nights leading up to a big exam. They try to override the relaxation signal by pouring in another cup of coffee and trying even harder to make themselves focus. This creates an ongoing battle between you and your body's natural energy cycles—and over time, your body will always win that battle.

So in those moments when you find yourself beginning to lose focus and you feel like you want to do anything but study, if you allow yourself a short break of as little as five minutes (but no more than twenty minutes), you will return to your studies refreshed and alert.

The Only Four Problems You Will Ever Face

Whatever the subject matter of the exam you are studying for, in the end it will involve one or more of these four types of problem in some combination:

1. Memory Tests

Many examinations are essentially memory tests. You will be asked to remember key dates from history, lists of vocabulary words in French, or stopping distances from driver's ed.

Fortunately, you now know how to do this. Using the "memory palace" you began creating in Chapter 8, along with the power of vivid associations, you will be able to remember long lists of facts and figures and recall them easily when the time comes to take your examination.

Be sure to give yourself time to really "install" the facts into your memory and practice recalling them a number of times before the actual exam. You can also create mind maps to get a clearer sense of how the things you are memorizing fit together and create new associations between them.

As with everything else to do with learning, deliberate practice makes perfect!

2. Problem-Solving

Most math and many science tests involve at least a section of problem-solving, where you will be given equations or word problems and asked to devise a solution. While occasionally the problems will be abstract and will call on you to use your spatial, verbal, or logical intelligence, more often than not your ability to solve the problems given will be down to your ability to choose the right formula and to apply it correctly.

While you will ultimately find your own preferred way to do this, a simple way to get started is to note each relevant formula on its own note card. Use an egg timer or the countdown timer on your phone and practice each formula for 5, 10, or 15 minutes at a time. When the timer goes off, move on to the next formula, being sure to build in breaks every 90 minutes or so to take advantage of your body's ultradian rhythms.

3. Creative Writing

Another common type of exam question is the written essay or oral examination—a chance to share your knowledge and insights into a subject. What will best prepare you for an essay-style exam is a deeper understanding of the material, as opposed to simply memorizing more facts. A simple way to go deeper into any subject is to begin by looking over any available materials until you have a sense of which source materials will be of most use to you. Then you can use a system of chunking I call the "pyramid of understanding" . . .

THE PYRAMID OF UNDERSTANDING

Read the technique all the way through before you start.

1. Get some index cards. As a rule, I use one card per chapter or article, but you can use more or fewer depending on the volume and depth of the material you are studying.

2. Go back through one section of your study materials, jotting down the key ideas for that chapter or section on your index card. The rule of thumb is no more than seven key ideas per card, though I prefer as few as three to five.

3. Now take a look at the card you have just written. If you were going to sum up the key ideas on the card in one word, phrase, or sentence, what would it be? Write your new key word, phrase, or sentence on the back side of the card.

4. Repeat steps 2 and 3 until you have completed cards for all your source material, then lay them out in a line with the summary side face up as in the illustration overleaf. This row of cards will become the bottom of your "pyramid."

5. Now, for every two to three cards, chunk up even further by coming up with a word, phrase, or sentence that sums up these key ideas. (*See the example overleaf to make this clearer.*) These new summary cards will become the second row of your "pyramid."

6. Continue chunking up, two to three cards at a time, until you have summed up the key idea behind the entire book or article in one word, phrase, or sentence.

From now on, whenever you want to review the material you can begin with the summary card and work your way back down into as much detail as you have time for. Always finish your study session by chunking all the way back up to the summary or essence of what you are studying.

Here is an example of how this strategy might be employed to study the first five chapters of this book:

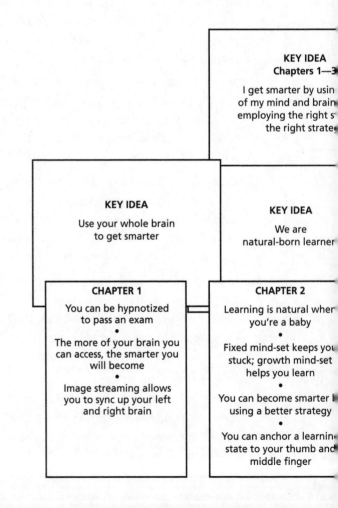

KEY IDEA
Chapters 1—3

I get smarter by usin
of my mind and brain
employing the right s
the right strate

KEY IDEA

Use your whole brain
to get smarter

KEY IDEA

We are
natural-born learner

CHAPTER 1

You can be hypnotized
to pass an exam
•
The more of your brain you
can access, the smarter you
will become
•
Image streaming allows
you to sync up your left
and right brain

CHAPTER 2

Learning is natural wher
you're a baby
•
Fixed mind-set keeps you
stuck; growth mind-set
helps you learn
•
You can become smarter
using a better strategy
•
You can anchor a learnin
state to your thumb and
middle finger

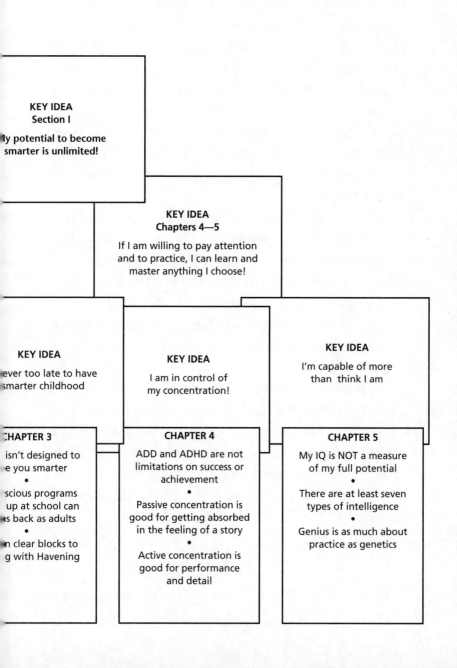

KEY IDEA
Section I

ly potential to become
smarter is unlimited!

KEY IDEA
Chapters 4—5

If I am willing to pay attention
and to practice, I can learn and
master anything I choose!

KEY IDEA

ever too late to have
smarter childhood

KEY IDEA

I am in control of
my concentration!

KEY IDEA

I'm capable of more
than think I am

CHAPTER 3

isn't designed to
e you smarter
•
scious programs
up at school can
s back as adults
•
n clear blocks to
g with Havening

CHAPTER 4

ADD and ADHD are not
limitations on success or
achievement
•
Passive concentration is
good for getting absorbed
in the feeling of a story
•
Active concentration is
good for performance
and detail

CHAPTER 5

My IQ is NOT a measure
of my full potential
•
There are at least seven
types of intelligence
•
Genius is as much about
practice as genetics

4. Practical demonstration of skill

In the 1960s, Professor L. V. Clark of Wayne State University did a study on the "effect of mental practice on the development of a certain motor skill." For the purposes of the study, he took two groups of high school basketball players and worked with them over a two-week period. One group practiced shooting free throws in the morning; the other group visualized shooting free throws, but did not do any practice. Clark found that both groups were able to improve their free throw shooting.

Further studies have shown that the optimal practice strategy is a combination of mental rehearsal and physical repetition, serving to develop both the relevant neural pathways in the mind and the appropriate "muscle memory" in the body.

You can use the "Modeling Excellence" exercise from Chapter 6 to assist you with the mental rehearsal part of your practice.

Of course, when you are preparing for any skill-based examination, the most important thing is to make sure that you are actually competent at the skill being tested. Until that point, anything I could teach you to make it more likely for you to pass the exam would be a disservice to both you and the community at large!

STEP TWO OF THREE: BEING IN THE RIGHT STATE WHEN IT REALLY MATTERS

The number one strategy I can give you for being in the right state when it really matters is to listen to the "Exam Confidence" hypnotic trance repeatedly in the days leading up to your exam. Some students like to play it on their mp3 player as the final step in their preparations before walking into the examination room to begin.

The following exercise will help prepare your mind to get the most out of the hypnotic trance. You can also use it on its own to ensure that you will be in a strong, confident, and resourceful state of mind when you need it most.

YOUR IDEAL EXAM PERFORMANCE STATE

Read the technique all the way through before you start.

1. Think about the very next exam you are going to be taking. If you don't have any exams scheduled, think about any upcoming performance situation where you want to be at your best.

2. If it was entirely up to you, how would you like to feel during your exam or performance?
    Example: *Relaxed, confident, focused, and creative*

3. Imagine a circle on the floor, of any color. Fill it up with the feelings you desire. You can do this by thinking of a time you felt that way in the past or by using your body "as if" you already feel that way now.
    Example: *I fill my circle with relaxed confidence by standing in a relaxed, confident posture and speaking to myself in an easy, confident tone of voice. I create a sense of focus by thinking about a time I felt extremely focused on what I was doing and vividly imagining it until I can feel those focused feelings in my body, then I add them into the circle. Finally, I crank up the slider on my creative force and put that into the mix as well!*

4. Step into the circle and let the feelings spread through your body. As you feel them, visualize yourself taking the exams, doing well, and handling unexpected challenges with ease. When the feelings start to fade, step out of the circle and "recharge" it with positive emotion, then step back in.

5. Repeat steps 3 and 4 until you automatically feel the way you want to feel while imagining taking your exams!

STEP THREE OF THREE: EXAM STRATEGY
The Seven Habits of Highly Successful Exam Takers

Remember, the only three things you need to learn anything are to be in the right state, to use the right strategy, and to practice, practice, practice! But when it comes to creating exam success, the moment arrives when practice is over and it's time to perform.

By practicing the seven strategies of highly successful exam takers I am going to share with you now, you will create habits of peak performance excellence that will serve you throughout the rest of your adult life.

1. Get a good night's sleep!

Providing you have attended the classes and read the required materials, a good night's sleep may be as powerful a study aid as an all-night cramming session. As you will discover in Chapter 14, sleep is a powerful ally in your quest for exam success.

2. Trust your preparation

A friend of mine once told me the story of the first time she planted a sunflower seed in hopes of growing a flower. Each day she would dig it back up to see if it had started to grow yet, not realizing that by doing so, she was actually preventing it from really taking root.

In the same way, once you step into the exam room, there's no need for an umpteenth "final" review—you're ready to go, and you're going to do just fine.

3. Take ownership of your environment

Diplomats and soldiers in high-risk environments are taught that one of the keys to surviving a hostage situation is to "take ownership of your environment"— that rather than fight against the less-than-optimal conditions you will no doubt find yourself in, you should make it your own as if you'd chosen to be there of your own accord. In the same way, successful test takers "dress for success" by wearing clothes they feel good in. They also make themselves at home in the exam-room environment, "decorating" their desk or place at the exam table with favorite knickknacks or anything else that makes them feel comfortable and at ease.

4. Read the instructions in their entirety

One of the things teachers often tell me is that a huge percentage of exam mistakes could be avoided if students simply read through all the instructions carefully before they began. If you want to experience the value of following instructions, on the next page is a practice test for you to do right now. Read through the instructions in their entirety before you begin . . .

1. Get a blank piece of paper and a pencil with an eraser.

2. On the first line on the paper, write the numbers 1 to 9. Be sure to leave a space between each number.

3. Circle the numbers 1, 2, 3, 5, and 7.

4. Place a square around each of the remaining numbers.

5. Write your name in the upper right-hand corner of the page.

6. Ignore steps 1 to 5 and continue reading.

If you read the instructions in their entirety, you saved yourself a lot of time and trouble. If not, you will almost certainly remember to do so from now on!

5. Look over the exam and do the easy stuff first

As you learned in Chapter 7, your mind is a self-organizing mechanism. In the same way as previewing a book allows your mind to spot patterns and "know where to look" for answers, looking over the exam before getting started will prime your mind for success. You can then either consciously plan how much time to allot to each section or you can allow your unconscious to instinctively apportion the time as you go.

You are then going to go through the entire exam three times. For your first pass, only respond to the questions or problems you can answer quickly and easily. In this way, you create a pattern of success and ensure at the very least you will get credit for all the questions you actually know the answer to.

6. Go back and do the difficult stuff second

After you have answered all the "no brainer" questions, go back to the beginning of the exam and work your way through the problems that take more time, thought, and effort. You should spend no more than three minutes on any one question before you begin to answer it (or outline your answer, if it's an essay question). If you get well and truly stuck, leave that question for now and move on.

7. When in doubt, "ask the teacher"

My absolute favorite trick for creating exam success is the "ask the teacher" technique. It is a kind of "guided guessing" that you can use on your third and final pass through the examination paper. Do this towards the end of the exam when you have answered all the easy questions, gone back and worked through the harder questions, and still have a bit of time left.

When you get to one of the remaining questions or problems and you cannot for the life of you find the answer in your own memory banks or by following your formulas, try this:

a. Close your eyes and imagine your teacher is standing in front of you.

b. In your mind's eye, ask them for the answer to the question.

c. If you don't get an answer, "step in" to your teacher so you're seeing through their eyes and look at the question again. You will be amazed at how often the answer comes to you!

Obviously, if you are taking an exam where you get points taken off for wrong answers, you may want to skip this step. But otherwise, give it a try! You have nothing to lose and everything to gain.

Moving Forward

We have now come to the end of Section II of the book. In Section III, you will learn strategies for creativity, problem-solving, smarter decisions, and staying sharp at any age. Until then, enjoy the chapter review and mind map on the following pages . . .

THE WHOLE CHAPTER IN ONE PAGE

- Exam success is $1/3$ study, $1/3$ state, and $1/3$ strategy.

- When studying, be sure to take ultradian rhythms into account. Take breaks of 5 to 20 minutes for every 90 minutes or so of study time.

- There are four types of problems in exams— memory tests, problem-solving, creative writing, and practical demonstration of skills. Each problem type has its own optimal study strategy.

- One of the best ways to prepare for your exam is to listen to the "Exam Confidence" hypnotic trance repeatedly in the days and nights leading up to the test. You can also do the "Ideal Exam Performance State" exercise to create an association between the exam and being at your best when it matters most.

- On exam day, it's important to trust your preparation and optimize your environment before you begin.

- Before doing anything else, read through all the instructions in their entirety and then look over the entire exam.

- You will then go through the exam three times—first to answer the easy questions, then to work through the difficult ones, and finally to guess at the answers to the ones you don't know. You can increase your chances of successful guessing by using the "Ask the Teacher" technique!

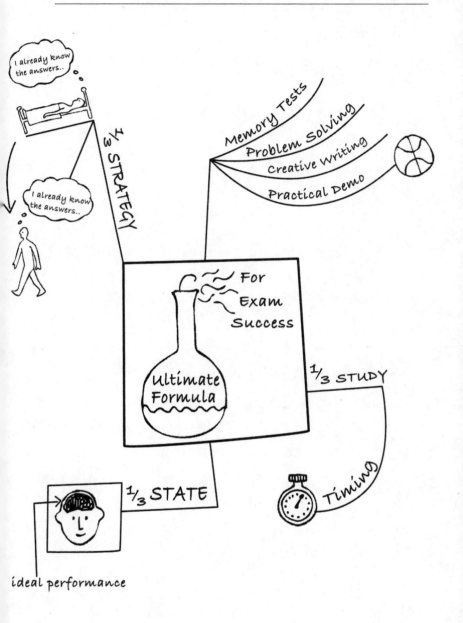

•

SMARTER
FOR LIFE

In Section III of this book, you'll learn the strategies of some of the most creative people alive. Soon, you'll be able to access that exact same creativity inside yourself and use it both to create new things in your life and to make smarter decisions and solve problems in the way that a creative genius might solve them.

Finally, I will show you not only how to develop your brain's capacity over time, but also what it takes to stay sharp at any age. In the final chapter I'll walk you through a daily brain workout that will help ensure you get smarter and smarter for life . . .

GET INTO THE ZONE!

Before you begin to read this chapter, check in to see if you are in your learning zone. If not, follow the steps below:

1. Take three slow and gentle breaths. Allow your body to relax and feel good.

2. Squeeze your thumb and middle finger together, firing off your "natural learning" anchor until you can begin to feel yourself going into a relaxed state of absorbed fascination.

3. Now, imagine what you would look like if you were just a little bit smarter than you are right now. How would you sit? What kind of expression would you have on your face? How would that smarter you show up in the world? How would they smile and interact with other people?

4. Step in to that smarter you so that you're seeing what they see, hearing what they hear, and feeling the way that they feel.

5. Set your concentration slider to the perfect blend of passive and active attention.

When you are ready, begin . . .

CHAPTER 11

•

You Are Creative!

The Creative Force

A number of years ago, one of the world's greatest songwriters contacted me because for the first time in his career he was having a problem with his creativity. It wasn't that he couldn't be creative—it's that he had no control over where or when his creativity would strike.

He'd go into the studio in the morning to compose a song and nothing would come. He couldn't get inspired. Then, at odd times, like in the evening just before a dinner party or in the middle of the night while he was trying to sleep, he'd suddenly get inspired and have to get to the piano and write quickly "before the song went away."

While the songs were still coming, the way they were coming was completely disrupting his life. So he asked me a very interesting question:

"Is there a way to turn creativity on and off?"

In thinking about that question, it became clear to me that "creativity" is just a neurophysiological state. In the same way that anger, fear, apathy, joy are all the product of how we are using our neurology and physiology in any given moment, creativity is a state where we have seemingly unlimited access to our greatest potential. In this state, we get insights, we have vision, we can become highly expressive, and think of innovative ideas. And since we're the ones creating the state through the way we're using our body and mind, we should be able to access it at will.

Notice that I'm not suggesting we control the content of our creativity. In fact, very often, creative people have told me it's almost as though they are channeling an idea, or I've heard them say that they feel like they're taking notes, that the idea is coming through them, rather than emanating from within them. But we are the ones creating the space for those creative ideas to flow through us and the state of mind and body where we will be most receptive to them.

So, I did a simple negotiation with this great songwriter's mind. We first of all had a conversation and I said, "When you're creative, what does it feel like?"

He said, "It feels like a kind of a force is coming through me, a force of creativity."

I said, "Well, I'm going to assume there's such a thing then, there's a creative force that you have access to. Let's play a game of creative imagination—could I talk to the force? Just remember some times when you were highly creative to bring it forward—it's okay if it feels like you're making it up."

And he said, "Yes, it feels like I'm in touch with the force now, and it says it's okay if you want to speak with it."

Now remember that the mind is infinitely creative. So when I asked the songwriter if I might speak to the creative force, I was simply speaking to that part of his mind that was responsible for his creativity.

So I said to the creative force, "I know that you have a positive intent and that you do a good job for our man, but you keep showing up at these times that are rather erratic. Would it be okay for you to show up at times when it was very convenient for him? Or could he have an on/off switch?"

And he said, "Yes, it feels like it's possible but I don't know how I'd do that."

"Right now, on a scale of 1 to 100, how creative do you feel?"

"I feel I'm at about 30 to 40."

"Could you take it to 50?"

He thought about it for a minute and replied, "Yes."

"Just remember times you were very creative, remember those now and that'll help."

"Yeah."

"Could you take it to 60?"

"Yes."

"To 70? 80? 90? 100?"

He said, "Oh my God, I want to write a song right now!"

Now if he had had writer's block and our goal had been to unblock his creativity, we could have stopped there. But what he really needed was control.

So I suggested to him that if the force could take itself up to 100, it could take itself back down again as well.

He said, "Yeah, the force could take it back down again," and down we went to 90, 80, 70, 60, 50, 40, and all the way back to a level where he knew the creative force was still available to him but was no longer in control of him.

We repeated the process a few times and then built a lever in his mind as a way of going in and out of that creative state, like the concentration slider you learned to build in Chapter 4. Then, just for fun, we cranked the creative force all the way up to 110—more creative than he'd ever been, and imagined sitting down at the piano with the force cranked up so it would be there when he most needed it. His face was almost glowing. In the end, he was almost chasing me out the door so he could get to his piano and begin writing.

Since that session, I've repeated the process with writers, artists, inventors, and business leaders. And before the end of this chapter, I will repeat the process with you!

We are going to create a "creativity slider" for you that you will be able to use to unleash the creative force in your own life.

But first, let's take a look at why that creative force may not have been as active in your life up to this point as it was when you were a child . . .

Recognizing Your Natural Creativity

You've probably heard the phrase "thinking outside the box," a skill sometimes called "lateral" or "divergent" thinking. For example, if I ask someone how many uses they can think of for an elastic band, they will generally come up with eight to ten, ranging from "holding a deck of cards together" to "shooting them at my friends." Someone who is very practiced in divergent thinking will come up with over 100 uses, because they will question everything from the size of the elastic band (what uses could you think of if the elastic band was 30 feet wide?) to the material it's made from (imagine what kind of slingshot you could build with an elastic band made from military-grade surgical tubing).

What's interesting is that in our society, the most divergent thinkers tend to be under the age of six. In one study, fully 98 percent of kindergarten children scored at a genius level for divergent thinking; five years later, aged ten to twelve, fewer than 50 percent scored as highly. The problem is not genetic—there are no changes in the brain that would account for those kinds of differences. More probably, these children are suffering from too much education.

Our education system is designed to cultivate critical thinking—and this is a truly important skill. Without it, we would all blindly rush ahead and pursue whatever hare-brained scheme popped into our heads, and the resultant chaos would make today's problems seem tame in comparison. But if all we have is critical thinking, nothing gets done. And as the saying goes, "The people who say it can't be done need to get out of the way of the people who are doing it."

Creativity, as far as I'm concerned, is any kind of thinking that leads to or contributes to the creation of a result. So creativity doesn't have to mean composing a symphony, or a screenplay, or a hit song. Writing an essay at school is a creative act. Finding a way to communicate with your teenagers is a creative act. Solving a problem at work is a creative act.

Basically, anything you do that addresses a problem or leads to the creation of something new in the world, no matter how small, is a creative act. Which means that unless you've been living under a rock for the past 20 years, you are already creative.

I know that some people have a little resistance to this idea, arguing that they're "not the creative type." This kind of prejudice assumes that somehow having long hair or wearing jeans switches on the creative juices and wearing a suit switches them off.

But the only real limit on your creativity is your willingness to recognize it and put it to work for you. That doesn't mean you will suddenly be able to write songs if you don't know music or to paint masterpieces if you've never picked up a brush. It just means that you can tap into the creative force whenever and wherever you want to solve problems and create new possibilities in your life and work.

The Wonderful World of Innovation

Walt Disney was one of the most creative and innovative geniuses of the 20th century. He didn't just introduce the world to characters like Mickey Mouse and Donald Duck—he also introduced the first feature-length animated film, *Snow White*, and with the purchase of some unused orchards in Orange County, California, created the first major theme park, Disneyland.

Today, the fruits of Disney's creativity are all around us. While he himself is gone, a leading expert in NLP named Robert Dilts used the NLP modeling strategies to gain a deeper insight into Disney's creativity.

One of the first things Dilts discovered was that people talked about "three Walt Disneys—the dreamer, the realist, and the spoiler." And apparently you never knew which one would walk into a meeting.

Sometimes, Walt the dreamer would come in, eyes to the sky, and he would begin daydreaming aloud about ideas for new characters and new possibilities for the company. Then all the other executives would dutifully begin to daydream and Walt the Realist would show up, insisting that they back up their dreams with practical actions and cost analyses until a step-by-step plan was in place and daily actions had begun.

But of course, just when the executives delivered their practical plans, Walt the Spoiler would take them into a room he called "the sweat box" and rip the plan to shreds, pointing out all the potential downsides, and insisting there would be no moving forward until every risk had been mitigated and every hole had been plugged.

What Dr. Dilts recognized was that the power of Disney's creativity strategy is that it makes full and separate use of the three stages of any creative process—daydreaming about possibility, taking practical action, and making space for a healthy critique of the process, interrogating it to ensure that what's being created is worth creating.

And it also addresses the primary block to our effective creative output—not that we don't know how to dream, be practical, or do downside planning, but that we so often attempt to do all three at the same time, shooting down our ideas before they're even fully formed in our own mind. The strategy developed by Dr. Dilts is simple, and involves separating out the three stages of the creative process so that you can maximize the impact of each while also benefiting from the synergy between them.

Think of the three aspects of Walt Disney's personality as three separate characters. The first is the **dreamer**—the person for whom all things are possible. You might think about someone who is a role model of possibility for you in this area—Leonardo da Vinci, Steven Spielberg, Anita Roddick, or Lady Gaga—anyone who for you represents the pure, full creative possibility of being alive.

Next up is the **realist**—the person who sorts things out. Again, take some time to identify one or two role models of efficiency and practical action. Imagine how they might approach your project if they were hired as a "project manager."

Finally, you have the **critic**, or spoiler. This is the pessimist—the person who sees problems where others see opportunities and who can seemingly always spot the flaw in a plan or the bits that just don't fit. Far from being an obstacle to creativity, the importance of listening to the critic is to ensure that your creative ideas don't enter into the world half-baked and you don't have to go back to the drawing board too early in the game.

I cannot say this strongly enough—if you are willing to employ your inner critic to help spot problems at the right point in the creative process, it will prove to be your biggest asset in producing wonderful new results in the world.

The process you are about to learn has helped people I've worked with to have amazing insights and creative ideas that have led to great success, riches, and fame. I use it myself while developing my stage and television programs, and I recommend it highly . . .

THE DISNEY CREATIVITY STRATEGY

Read the technique all the way through before you start.

1. Choose four spaces to work with—it can be four different rooms in your home, four different seats at your kitchen table, or even four different environments, like a park, a café, your office, and your home.

2. Decide which space will be your "**dreaming**" space. For you as the dreamer, all things are possible and nothing is off-limits. Go there and take some time to actively daydream about something you'd like to create in your life or in the world. There are no restrictions and no limits here—no matter how outrageous or "unrealistic" your idea may seem, have fun exploring the possibilities.

   Here are some useful questions for you to consider:

   • What would you love to have happen?
   • What would you attempt if you knew you couldn't fail?
   • What will having that happen get you or give you?
   • What would 100 percent success look, feel, and sound like?
   • If you could wave a magic wand and have things turn out exactly the way that you wanted, what would you wave your magic wand for?

   If any practical considerations occur to you, leave them for now—rest assured, you will get to them later!

Continued

3. When you're ready, move to your **"realist"** space. Now is the time to get practical. You're not trying to evaluate the value or even the feasibility of your idea—simply assume that you are going to go forward with it and figure out exactly what it will take to make things happen. You might work out costs, calculate timing, and whatever else would have to happen in order for what you want to create to be created.

   Here are some useful questions to get you started:

   • What actually needs to be done?
   • Who else needs to be involved? How much will it cost?
   • How will we know when our goal has been achieved?
   • What are the relevant time constraints?
   • When and where will each phase be carried out?
     Again, leave any further daydreams about possibilities or evaluations about how worthwhile the project may be until later—this space is just for going through the practicalities of your creation.

4. It's time to move to the space of the **critic**, the "sweat box." This is your time to let all the negativity and reasons why you can't create come to the table. Here are some useful questions for this stage of the process:

   • How do all the elements of this idea fit together? What bits appear unbalanced?

- Why is each step necessary? Is there anything that does not fit with the overall objective of the project?
- What parts of the project are underdeveloped or not fully thought through?
- How possible is this within the time frame you have allotted?
- What are the potential consequences if the plan fails? Are you prepared to handle those consequences?

      It's important to remember that you are not being judged here—but your creative daydream is. This is where you can let your internal critic go wild!

5. Step out of the "sweat box" and into the fourth space, the **neutral** area. You should now have a clear sense of what you would like to create, how specifically it could be created, and what problems are likely to arise along the way.

6. When you're ready, return to the space of the **dreamer** and allow yourself to daydream possible creative solutions to each of the problems on your list. You may find the strategies in Chapter 12, for solving problems like a genius, to be extremely useful here.

7. Back to the space of the **realist**. What's the practical reality of implementing those solutions? How specifically will you go about doing it?

Continued

8. Now to the space of the **critic**. Why won't these solutions work? What's likely to go wrong? What's the bottom line?

9. Continue to cycle through the **dreamer, realist, and critic** phases of the process until one of two things happen:

   a. You recognize that this idea is impractical or undesirable for you to pursue, at least for now.

   b. Your inner critic has been silenced. When your own internal judge has ruled in favor of your idea or plan, you know you're on to a winner!

Of course, you don't always have to use four separate spaces once you get the hang of the idea. One writer I worked with who had been suffering from writer's block bought himself three hats and would switch headgear whenever he made the move from outlining (dreamer) to writing (realist) to editing (critic). He said it really helped him remember not to edit while he was putting words on the page, and that he hasn't really become stuck in his work since.

However you wind up using it, remember the basic idea is a simple one—when you're dreaming, dream; when you're judging, judge; and when you're creating, create!

Harnessing the Creative Force

Let's finish this chapter by going through the technique I described to you at the beginning: installing a slider that will allow you to harness your full creativity whenever and wherever you want it most. The more time you take to go through each step in vivid detail, the more powerfully it will work. Each time you listen to the "Smarter While You Sleep" hypnotic trance, your creative abilities will be enhanced and reinforced . . .

THE CREATIVITY BOOSTER

Read the technique all the way through before you start.

1. Close your eyes and think of a time when you were creative. It could be in the office or at home; in front of a computer or a blank canvas; on a sports field or playing cards.

2. Return to that time like you are back there again now. See what you saw, hear what you heard, and get in touch with that feeling of creativity.

3. Now notice where you feel the creative feeling strongest in your body. Is it in your head? Your chest? Stomach? Arms, hands, or fingers?

4. Wherever that feeling is already at its strongest, give it a color and imagine that color spreading up to the top of your head and down to the tips of your toes. Now make the color brighter and stronger and notice the feelings intensify.

5. Imagine that you can communicate with this creative force. Notice where it currently is on a scale from 1 to 100, where 1 is minimal creativity and 100 is you at your most creative.

6. Wherever it currently is, increase it by 10. Continue to increase it in small increments until it is all the way up to 100.

7. Once it reaches 100, ask it to move back down incrementally, first to 90, then 80, all the way back down to a level that feels comfortable for you.

8. Now imagine a slider like you would find on a mixing board or equalizer. Set the slider so that it matches your current level of creativity. Then once again ask your creative force to go up in increments of 10, this time moving the slider up in increments of 10 at the same time.

9. Continue to ask the creative force to move up and down the scale incrementally, being sure to move the slider up and down at the same time.

10. To test your new creativity booster, move the slider up and feel your access to the creative force increase; then move it back down and feel it decrease.

11. If you want regular access to your creativity in a particular setting or location, imagine yourself in that setting now and push the slider all the way up to 110— into a state of heightened creativity beyond anything you may yet have experienced. This will ensure that a new association is made between the creative force and your preferred "instrument" or place of creative expression.

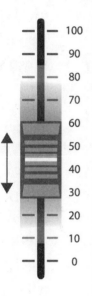

12. When you are finished, return your creativity booster to a comfortable level.

In the next chapter, I will show you how to use your creativity to solve problems like a genius. Until then, take a few moments to review the concepts in this chapter . . .

THE WHOLE CHAPTER IN ONE PAGE

- The creative force is available to all of us, once we learn to harness it and put it to use. Whatever it is you do and no matter your personality, you are creative!

- When we are young, we naturally think outside the box. As we become more "educated," we need to be more deliberate in separating out our capacities for creative, practical, and critical thinking.

- The Disney strategy is a simple tool you can use to make use of your full range of thinking and possibility.

- You can learn to evoke your creativity at will.

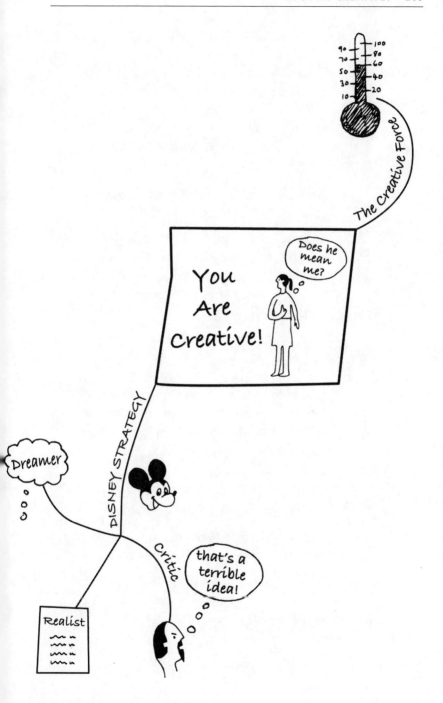

GET INTO THE ZONE!

Before you begin to read this chapter, check in to see if you are in your learning zone. If not, follow the steps below:

1. Take three slow and gentle breaths. Allow your body to relax and feel good.

2. Squeeze your thumb and middle finger together, firing off your "natural learning" anchor until you can begin to feel yourself going into a relaxed state of absorbed fascination.

3. Now, imagine what you would look like if you were just a little bit smarter than you are right now. How would you sit? What kind of expression would you have on your face? How would that smarter you show up in the world? How would they smile and interact with other people?

4. Step in to that smarter you so that you're seeing what they see, hearing what they hear, and feeling the way that they feel.

5. Set your concentration slider to the perfect blend of passive and active attention.

6. Turn your creativity slider up high!

When you are ready, begin . . .

CHAPTER 12

•

Solve Problems
Like a Genius

Solving the Unsolvable

One of my favorite examples of the ability of the mind to solve literally *any* problem, which I have written about before, is the story of George Bernard Dantzig, a student who arrived late for a math class and saw two problems written on the blackboard. Assuming they were the day's homework, he jotted them down but found it took him longer than expected to actually solve them.

When he handed in his homework a few days late, his teacher seemed taken aback, and Dantzig quickly apologized, explaining that "they were a bit more difficult than usual."

The equations he had solved had not been meant as homework at all—they were two famously "unsolvable" problems of statistics. Because Dantzig didn't know he wasn't supposed to be able to solve them, he was able to bring the full power of his creative mind to the problems. His work was later published in academic papers and his story became legend.

The point is this:

When you tap into the genius and creativity of your mind, solving even the most difficult problems becomes possible.

Remember, the secret to mastering anything is to put yourself in the right state, to use an effective strategy, and to persist through trial and error until you have learned, achieved, or created whatever you set out to learn, achieve, or create. Since you already know how to get yourself into a highly creative state, in this chapter I am going to share three incredibly powerful problem-solving strategies that have been modeled from geniuses throughout history.

While a couple of them may seem a bit strange at first, the fact that they're "outside the box" of what people normally do is the very reason why they're so much more effective than conventional practices or techniques.

STRATEGY NUMBER ONE:
ASKING A BETTER QUESTION

There is a story that Albert Einstein was once asked what he would do if he was about to be killed and only had one hour to figure out how to save his life. He replied, "I would devote the first 55 minutes of that hour to searching for the right question. Once I have that question, finding the answer would only take about five minutes." I have long believed that Einstein came up with so many smart ideas because he was so relentless in asking himself smart questions.

While I'm no Einstein, over the years I've learned that a good question is worth its weight in gold. This is not only for the answers it draws forth but also for the positive frame of mind it can help you to get into.

The questions that follow are drawn from the work of Michael Gelb, who has done extensive research into the life of Leonardo da Vinci, widely regarded as the most complete genius in terms of multiple intelligences the world has ever known. Leonardo da Vinci was a great believer in the principle of *curiosità*—the idea of approaching life with insatiable curiosity and an unrelenting quest for continuous learning.

One way of tapping into your curiosity is by using the anchor for absorbed fascination you created in Chapter 2. Another is through the continual asking and answering of questions. Gelb proposes that almost any problem can be solved by the repeated asking of just seven questions—what, when, who, how, where, why, and what if . . . ?

In the section below, I have shared some of my favorite variations on these questions. In order to put these questions to work for you, simply choose a problem, concern, or worry, put yourself into a highly creative state, and answer as many of the following questions as honestly and completely as you can. Over time, you will discover your own favorites and can add them to the list . . .

THE SEVEN QUESTIONS

1. **What . . .**

   . . . is the essence of this problem?

   . . . are three positive things about this problem?

   . . . will it be like when this problem is completely solved?

2. **When . . .**

   . . . does it seem most like a problem?

   . . . does it seem least like a problem?

   . . . does it need to be resolved by?

3. **Who . . .**

   . . . created this problem?

   . . . would benefit most from this problem being solved?

   . . . could solve this problem most easily?

4. **How . . .**

   . . . could I get a fresh perspective on this problem?

   . . . will I know that this problem has been solved?

   . . . could I motivate myself to do what needs to be done to solve **this problem?**

5. **Where . . .**

   . . . doesn't it happen?

   . . . haven't I looked for answers yet?

   . . . else has this happened, in my life or in the world?

6. **Why . . .**

   . . . is resolving this problem important?
   . . . does this problem persist?
   . . . haven't I resolved it yet?

7. **What if . . .**

   . . . I knew I would discover the solution to this problem exactly one week from today—how would that change what I am doing now?
   . . . this turned out to be the best thing that ever happened to me. What then?
   . . . this was completely resolved by the end of today. What would I focus on next?

Each time you ask and answer these questions and other variations that occur to you, you will gain new insights into how to better handle the situation you are exploring.

STRATEGY NUMBER TWO:
SOLVING PROBLEMS BEFORE THEY HAPPEN

The anthropologist/philosopher Gregory Bateson, one of the true geniuses of the 20th century, used to tell the story of an entomologist at New College, Oxford, who discovered to his dismay that the huge oak beams across the top of the great dining hall were filled with beetles and beginning to rot. When he reported his findings to the college council, they were extremely dismayed, as the sheer size and quality of the beams made finding suitable replacements unlikely before the current ones gave way. Fortunately, word of this problem reached the college forester, whose job it was to tend to the many pieces of college-owned land scattered around the county.

He approached the council with some welcome news. Nearly 500 years earlier, at the time the original great hall was being built, the forward-thinking architect had insisted that a grove of oaks be planted on college land so they would be available to replace the beams when they eventually began to rot and give way. This plan had been passed down from forester to forester for hundreds of years, each one telling his successor, "You don't cut them oaks. Them's for the College Hall."

The ability to plan ahead and solve problems before they occur isn't solely the domain of architects or college foresters. Nikola Tesla, who developed the "alternating current" (AC) that characterizes nearly all of the commercial electrical supply in the world today, could design a machine in his mind with such precision that he was able to project into its future life and see where the machine would break down after months or even years of use. He would then use that information to improve the design of the machines, preventing problems before they even came into existence.

At a much more basic level, professional golfers imagine how the flight of their ball will be affected by the wind and adjust their swing accordingly, music producers adapt the mix of a record to optimize the sound for an iPod or car stereo, and fashion-conscious wedding guests can plan their outfit so it not only fits into the overall theme of the day but doesn't outshine the bride.

I use this same ability to do what Einstein called a "thought experiment" to assist me in the writing of all my books. I project out into the future and imagine holding the finished book in my hands. I can "see" the cover, feel the pages, and sense the outline, flow, and design of the overall book. Sometimes, I will ask myself questions about the book that serve to sharpen my "future vision" and make clear what's still missing or what might need to be changed.

Over the years I have had the opportunity to work with some of the leading screenwriters in Hollywood. I take them through a process where I ask them to go to an imaginary screening room in the future and watch the movie they are currently writing up on the screen, as if it had already been made. Often they can't yet see the whole movie, so I ask them just to sense the emotional tone of it and in particular get a feel for the beginning, middle, and end. Before long, they start to see flashes of individual scenes. Each time they repeat the process, they get even more details of what works and where the potential problems are. By the time we have finished, they are often able to rewrite several scenes based on what they have "seen" in the future.

To use this strategy for yourself, think about a project you are currently working on or a problem you are trying to solve. The project might be a proposal you are putting together at work, a relationship you are thinking about taking to the next level, or a creative project you are developing for the future. If you choose to explore a problem, it can be anything that will have a specific resolution at some point in the future.

When you have a specific project or problem in mind, read through the following process in its entirety and then close your eyes and do the thought experiment for yourself . . .

BACK FROM THE FUTURE

Read the technique all the way through before you start.

1. Take a couple of deep breaths and relax. Give yourself the time and space to really enjoy this process.

2. When you're ready, imagine that the project you have chosen to explore is already complete or the problem you are trying to solve has been resolved. Project yourself forward in time so you are there at the moment of completion or resolution. Notice what you notice. Do your best to involve all your senses—imagine not only what you will see, but what you can hear, touch, taste, and smell.

3. Ask questions of the you that is now in the future. While you will come up with your own favorites, here are some of mine:
   • What's the best thing about this?
   • What would be even better?
   • What's not yet the way you want it?

4. Having now completed this project or solved this problem, what do you know now that you wish you'd known when you were starting out?

5. When you feel a sense of greater clarity, come fully back to the present, bringing the energy of successful completion and resolution back with you. Be sure to make notes about what you've learned, and implement any changes or improvements that occurred to you during the process just as soon as you can!

STRATEGY NUMBER THREE: YOUR GENIUS MASTERMIND

One of the most common strategies for problem-solving that is sometimes easy to overlook is the power of sharing your problem with one or more people and asking them to assist you in generating creative solutions. It can be a partner or parent, coach, colleague, or friend. What's important is that it's someone you feel will not judge you for having the problem and who you feel comfortable exploring solutions with.

Of course, sometimes the people you spend time with get bogged down in the same kind of problematic thinking that you do. When that happens, I encourage you to turn to something I call your "inner mastermind."

To get a sense for how this actually works, think about the biggest problem you are currently facing in your life or work. Now ask yourself, if you could consult anyone in the world for advice on this, who would you choose? What advice do you think they would give you?

The idea of an inner mastermind is to create an "inner council" of advisors with whom you can explore your biggest problems and gain insights into possible solutions. Think about it for yourself. What if you could have Richard Branson and Bill Gates as business mentors? Imagine how many problems you could solve if Albert Einstein and Sherlock Holmes were on your creative team. And what if you could have Shakespeare, Cleopatra, or someone else of your choosing to help you with matters of the heart?

In order to facilitate this process, we do an exercise on my seminars where participants "step in" to a role model or someone they want to learn from. In order to do this effectively, it is simply necessary to be very familiar with that person's work. Ideally each participant will have some first-hand experience of their chosen role model, but since in many cases that's not possible it helps if they have read numerous books by or about them, watched multiple videos and/or listened to recordings of them speaking.

When it's time to do the "genius step in," we ask the participants to "become" the person they have chosen, a bit like when a method actor fully immerses himself or herself into a character. Some people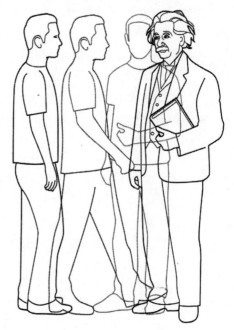
find it helps to get the
body posture first,
by imagining they
are standing in front
of their role model.
They then physi-
cally step into them,
beginning to move
their body the way
that person moves,
and to speak the way
they speak.

The results are always amazing and often very funny. In doing what seems at first like a simple impersonation, they become more confident, optimistic, creative, or intelligent. It's as though by taking on the physiology and speech of the person, they gain access to the same quality of thinking.

What I've learned over the years is that you can use a very basic version of this technique to gain a new perspective or insight into any problem area you would like to explore. It involves "stepping in" to the perspective of somebody who is skilled at the area you are exploring, and then looking at your present situation "through their eyes." As an extra twist, in the "inner mastermind" we incorporate the element of using multiple role models to deepen the possibility of our receiving useful insights and solutions.

To practice this strategy for yourself, choose three to six people to have as part of your inner mastermind, and at least one problem or question to explore. Be sure that these are people you both admire and respect . . .

A MEETING OF THE MINDS

Read the technique all the way through before you start.

1. Close your eyes and imagine that the people you would most like to ask for advice about your problem are standing or sitting in front of you.

2. In your imagination, float into their bodies one by one, "seeing" your problem through their eyes and noticing what insights come to mind.

3. If you have any specific questions, be sure to ask them. You may be surprised by the answers!

4. After you have explored your situation from each role model's point of view, allow them to interact with one another in your imagination. Sometimes these "discussions" lead to valuable additional insights and solutions.

5. Take action on your best insights as soon as you possibly can.

Don't worry if this feels a bit strange at first—the more you do it the easier and more natural it becomes!

In the next chapter, I will show you how to make smarter decisions by using your whole brain and the wisdom of your unconscious. Until then, enjoy this review of the core ideas, concepts, and strategies behind this chapter . . .

THE WHOLE CHAPTER IN ONE PAGE

- When you tap into the genius and creativity of your mind, solving even the most difficult problems becomes possible.

- Asking better questions will always lead to better answers. The seven most important questions you can ask are what, when, who, how, where why, and what if.

- It is often easier to solve a problem from the perspective of the future. You can take advantage of this fact by imagining yourself in the future now and seeing how much you already know about what to do.

- Sometimes, the best way to solve a problem isn't by looking at it in a different way, it's by looking at it through different eyes.

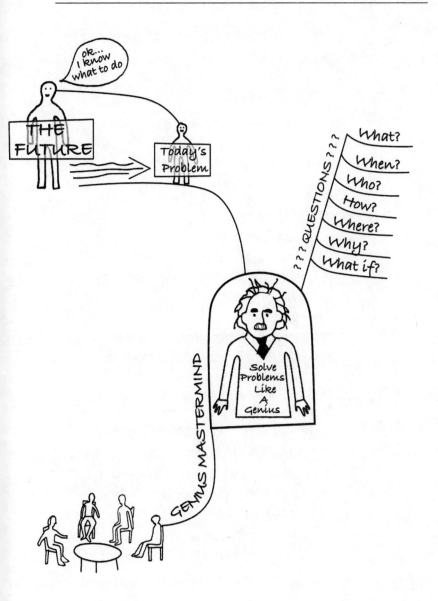

GET INTO THE ZONE!

Before you begin to read this chapter, check in to see if you are in your learning zone. If not, follow the steps below:

- Take three slow and gentle breaths. Allow your body to relax and feel good.

- Squeeze your thumb and middle finger together, firing off your "natural learning" anchor until you can begin to feel yourself going into a relaxed state of absorbed fascination.

- Now, imagine what you would look like if you were just a little bit smarter than you are right now. How would you sit? What kind of expression would you have on your face? How would that smarter you show up in the world? How would they smile and interact with other people?

- Step in to that smarter you so that you're seeing what they see, hearing what they hear, and feeling the way that they feel.

- Set your concentration slider to the perfect blend of passive and active attention.

- Turn your creativity slider up high!

When you are ready, begin . . .

CHAPTER 13

•

How to Make
Smarter Decisions

The Most Powerful Force in the Universe

I am going to begin this chapter with a bold statement:

**Your life is the sum total of every
decision you have made.**

Now that doesn't mean that if something terrible has happened to you, it's your fault. It just means that you have a remarkable influence over both your experience of life and how your life turns out. The decisions you're making right now about what's important, what to pay attention to, how to show up in the world, and how to approach both the positives and the negatives in your environment are the factors determining both the quality and the direction of your life.

There are, of course, people who are born with certain advantages—genetic, environmental, and financial—to give them a flying start. But there are also people who achieve against all odds. In fact, for most geniuses, defying the odds was where it started. Einstein was told by his teachers at school that he would never amount to anything. Stephen Hawking was told he would not live long enough even to finish his doctorate, let alone transform the world's understanding of time and cosmology. In short, it is not the cards you are dealt that determine how the game turns out—it's how you decide to play them.

At any moment in your life, you can make a decision. It's a basic sort of human right, if you like. And it's in these moments of decision that your destiny is created. What will you embrace, and what will you reject? What will you commit to?

The power to shape your life is inside you right now, waiting to be put to work. So one of the most important things you can learn to do is to ensure that the majority of decisions you make are good ones.

A Different Way to Work

Many high achievers do their jobs as if they are in a race with themselves to get somewhere, though when I ask them where it is they are trying to get in such a hurry they often don't know. Others spend their working hours trying to win the game of "who's the busiest?," rarely if ever stopping to see if what they are doing is truly productive or worthwhile.

By contrast, my friend Simon Cowell has a completely different approach to business. On a typical day he gets up, has breakfast, reads the papers, and gets himself into a great frame of mind. Then he looks to make one really good decision before the end of the day to move his business forward. He said to me that he would rather make one really good decision a day than 500 average ones.

Now, I know Simon is also a very hard worker—very few people could sustain his schedule and level of performance over time. But hearing him talk about the importance he places on making smarter decisions on a regular basis gave me insight into why he's been able to stay at the top of his game for so many years. And it's led to a change in the way I run my companies as well. Our motto is now simply this:

Work smarter, not harder.

As a result, we've been able to continue to grow and adapt to a changing marketplace with a minimum of stress or hardship.

A Simple Place to Start

The good news about decisions is that if we are willing to learn a bit more about how to make them, we can increase our success rate without ever risking any significant failure. This fits in with what nearly all of the truly successful entrepreneurs I have met have told me—that they don't do risk, they do *calculated* risk. And it turns out that most things just aren't as risky as they may seem at first glance.

Let's say you're thinking about starting your own business on the side as you wait and see what will become of your current employment. On the upside, it would give you extra income now and the possibility of completely replacing your job at some point in the future if it goes well. On the downside, it will take some work and a little bit of money to get started.

So the upside is an 8—greater flexibility now and the possibility of more freedom later. The downside is a 4—you could actually lose a little bit of money, but you've already done the math and know that if that did happen, you can afford it.

On the other hand, what if you'd worked out that you couldn't afford to lose that little bit of money— that it was the only buffer you had between losing your job and losing your home? Then the upside would be an 8 and the downside would be a 10. In that case, the smarter decision would be to look for a better opportunity, one that was more appropriate to your current circumstances.

CALL TO ACTION

Make five decisions a day

Make at least five conscious decisions a day, every day, for the next week. Write them down so you can keep track of how they work out. They can be as small as "shall I have tea or coffee?" or as large as you like. Be sure to check the upside and downside before making each decision. The point is simply to get the decision muscle working on the small stuff so that it will be fit for those times when you have larger decisions to make.

HOW TO MAKE SMARTER DECISIONS • 235

The Ultimate Decision Strategy

Remember, there are only three keys to being smarter in everything we do:

1. **Be in a "smarter" state.**

2. **Use a "smarter" strategy.**

3. **Keep on using the master strategy of trial and success until you create the results you desire.**

Each one of these applies equally well to making smarter decisions. When you are in a less-than-optimal state, the decisions you make are liable to be bad decisions. When you are in a better state, you will make better decisions. So a part of any effective decision strategy will be to make sure you are in a fit state to make the decision in the first place.

This is why some very smart people make some very stupid decisions.

Very few decisions are so genuinely urgent that they can't wait until you are in a better state to make them. And you already have the tools to go into a better state at your fingertips!

In this chapter, rather than share some abstract theory of decision making, I will help you to discover your ultimate strategy for making smarter decisions—the strategy you *already* use. In order to uncover that strategy, you are going to learn from decisions you have made in the past how to make smarter decisions now and in the future.

We've all made decisions that turned out for the best and other decisions that turned out badly. But the kinds of decisions we can really learn from are those times when we made a bad decision and we knew it was a bad decision even when we were making it, or we made a good decision that we knew was a good decision even at the time.

My friend Steven has been married for over 20 years. He told me how it happened: one day he realized that he had fallen in love with the girl who had been his best friend for over a year. But there was a problem. She was about to go to her graduation ball with someone else, and as far as she knew she and Steven were "just good friends." So he decided to declare his love for her the afternoon before the big dance. He could have been rejected. He could have embarrassed himself. He could even have ruined a wonderful friendship. But at some level he just knew it was the right thing to do.

To be fair, she didn't know what to make of his declaration, and she even told her girlfriends she was a little worried that Steven might have gone off the deep end. But something inside her clicked, and although she still went to the dance with the other guy, at the end of the night she came back home alone. Within a week, she and Steven were together and they've been happily together ever since.

Of course, sometimes the same thing happens in reverse. Early on in my career, I went into business with someone who many of my friends and several people in the business community warned me had a checkered past. Although I was concerned that so many people whose opinion I respected distrusted him, I was blinded by the stories he told about how much money we would make and how much fun we would have living the high life. While a part of me knew that going into business with him was probably a mistake, youthful enthusiasm and, if I'm being honest, a touch of greed had their way. While I did eventually learn my lesson, it was only after he had disappeared with the vast majority of our profits.

In a few moments, I will take you through a process originally created by Dr. Richard Bandler that will help attune your unconscious mind to making better decisions on a more consistent basis. In order to get the most out of this exercise, you will need to come up with at least one decision that at some level you knew was a good decision even when you were making it, and another that you at least suspected might be a bad decision at the time and turned out badly or worse. For the purposes of this exercise, the more obviously good or bad the decisions were to you at the time, the better.

I will then ask you a series of questions about the two decisions to help your brain calibrate, using the differences between them. Our brains code our memories in specific ways to make it easy for us to spot the difference between what we like and don't like, what works and what doesn't, and what we should move towards and what we need to move away from.

By going into the detail of your brain's coding and highlighting the differences between how it codes a good decision and how it codes a bad one, we are training our intuition to pay more attention to those differences so that it can spot them even earlier in the process and send us a stronger signal to either pull back or go full speed ahead.

As you do this exercise, you are telling your unconscious mind, "Look, that's how we do it when it doesn't work out—do less of that. This was a time we got it right. Do more of this!"

GOOD DECISION, BAD DECISION

Read the technique all the way through before you start.

1. Think about a time when you made a good decision and were pretty sure it was a good decision when you made it. When you think about it, notice what image or picture comes to mind. Now, regardless of the content of the picture, I want you to notice the following distinctions:
    *   Is the picture in front of you, to the left, or to the right?
    *   Big or small?
    *   Moving or still (i.e. like a movie or a photograph)?
    *   Focused or unfocused?
    *   Bright or dim?
    *   Are the images close, far away, or "like real life?"
    *   Do you see yourself in the picture or are you looking through your own eyes as if you were actually there?

2. Now notice what soundtrack is connected with this decision.
    *   Is it sounds, voices, or both?
    *   Loud or soft?
    *   In front of you, to the side, or behind you?

3. Finally, notice the feelings in your body as you think about this decision.
    *   Where in your body are you most aware of feelings?
    *   Are they tight or relaxed?
    *   Where do the feelings start? Where do they move to?

Continued

4. Stop and make a few notes about what you noticed. Circle any details that seemed particularly intense or significant.

5. Now, you are going to repeat the process for the bad decision. Think about the bad decision that you made, and notice how you are representing it in your mind. Begin with the images, and notice:
   - Is the picture in front of you, to the left, or to the right?
   - Big or small?
   - Moving or still (i.e. like a movie or a photograph)?
   - Focused or unfocused?
   - Bright or dim?
   - Are the images close, far away, or "like real life?"
   - Do you see yourself in the picture or are you looking through your own eyes as if you were actually there?

6. Now notice what soundtrack is connected with this decision.
   - Is it sounds, voices, or both?
   - Loud or soft?
   - In front of you, to the side, or behind you?

7. Finally, notice the feelings in your body as you think about this decision.
   - Where in your body are you most aware of feelings?
   - Are they tight or relaxed?
   - Where do the feelings start? Where do they move to?

8. Once again, take a few moments to jot down what you noticed, this time circling any details that were noticeably different from the way your brain thinks about the good decision.

9. Now, go back inside and compare the good decision and the bad decision side by side, noticing the differences in picture, sound, and feeling between the two. Keep flicking back and forth between the two until you have a clear sense of what a good decision looks, sounds, and feels like and what a bad decision looks, sounds, and feels like.

Used with the written permission of Dr. Richard Bandler

During the "Smarter while you Sleep" hypnotic trance, I will be asking your unconscious mind to amplify the signals of both kinds of decision. When you are about to make a good decision, you will have a stronger sense of familiarity, like an inner "Aha!" that lets you know you're on the right track. It will also amplify the warning signs of a bad decision, like an inner "Watch out—bad decision ahead!" that will make it easier for you to step back and choose more wisely.

Of course, nothing can prevent you from making decisions that don't work out the way you hoped. There are too many variables in the world for us to suddenly get everything just perfect and exactly the way that we want it. However, this process will allow you to increase your batting average. It ups the odds of making good decisions and decreases the odds of making bad ones. And that's just a smarter way to do things.

We're almost at the end of the book, and I hope you've found that taking the time to read through it and put the techniques into practice has been one of the smartest decisions you've ever made. Before we move on to strategies for keeping your brain in optimal health and staying sharp at any age, take a few moments to review the key points from this chapter . . .

THE WHOLE CHAPTER IN ONE PAGE

- **The power to make decisions is one of the greatest powers we all have. Our decisions determine both the quality and the direction of our lives.**

- **A single really good decision is likely to be more productive than a series of average ones.**

- **Most people who procrastinate aren't lazy—they're afraid of failing. You can mitigate your fear of failing by always calculating the upside and downside of any decision.**

- **One of the keys to making good decisions is being in a good state. If you are upset, nervous, angry, or frightened, it's not a good time to make a decision.**

- **At some level, we intuitively know the difference between a good decision and a bad decision. By looking deeper into those differences, we can train our intuition to make good decisions more often and avoid the bad ones.**

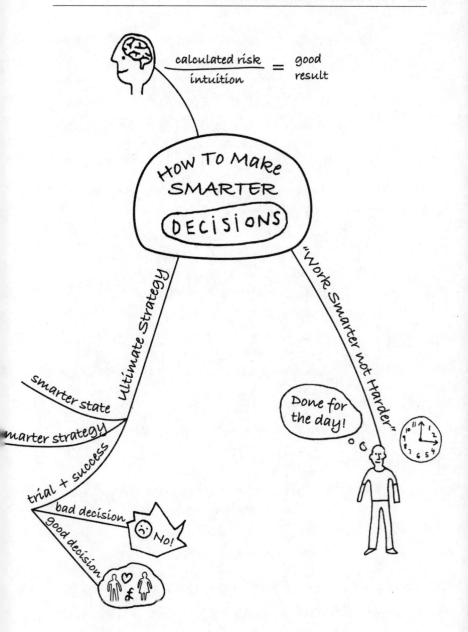

GET INTO THE ZONE!

Before you begin to read this chapter, check in to see if you are in your learning zone. If not, follow the steps below:

- Take three slow and gentle breaths. Allow your body to relax and feel good.

- Squeeze your thumb and middle finger together, firing off your "natural learning" anchor until you can begin to feel yourself going into a relaxed state of absorbed fascination.

- Now, imagine what you would look like if you were just a little bit smarter than you are right now. How would you sit? What kind of expression would you have on your face? How would that smarter you show up in the world? How would they smile and interact with other people?

- Step in to that smarter you so that you're seeing what they see, hearing what they hear, and feeling the way that they feel.

- Set your concentration slider to the perfect blend of passive and active attention.

- Turn your creativity slider up high!

When you are ready, begin . . .

CHAPTER 14

•

Staying Sharp
at Any Age

In Search of Einstein's Brain

In 1955, without permission from family or friends, the pathologist on duty at Albert Einstein's autopsy removed the great scientist's brain to see if he could find any physiological differences between Einstein's brain and that of a "normal" person. More than 20 years later, a neuroanatomist named Dr. Marilyn Diamond got hold of Einstein's brain and made a startling discovery.

While the majority of his brain was indistinguishable from that of any normal person, there were significantly more glial cells in his left parietal lobe. Glial cells are like cell phone towers inside your brain, transferring electrochemical signals between neurons. The more glial cells, the faster and more efficiently information will travel throughout the brain, making them a far more accurate indicator of potential brain power than the actual size of a brain or the number of neurons it contains, both of which are predetermined at birth.

Unlike neurons, which die off over time, glial cells can actually *increase* in number throughout your life. And what produces more glial cells is mental exercise. In short, when it comes to your brain, the rule of thumb is the same as when it comes to the musculature of your body:

Use it or lose it!

Although the brain's capacity to acquire knowledge and make new associations is very well-known, indeed is the basis of our education system, its ability to actually change its physical structure in response to new challenges is a fairly recent discovery. Simply put, the brain will adapt and change in response to specific challenges, in the same way as the muscles in the body will develop and strengthen in response to the physical demands of exercise and athletic challenges. This ability is called "neuroplasticity," and it has led to a virtual explosion of research into what will make our brains more efficient, effective, responsive, and resilient.

Dr. Ryuta Kawashima is a professor at Tohoku University in Japan who has been studying brain functioning for many years, using brain-imaging technology to measure how much of the brain is activated during different types of mental activity. What he found was that certain types of activities were dramatically more effective than others at engaging the brain and keeping it sharp.

Unsurprisingly, watching television is near the bottom of the list. But two activities you might associate with more active brain functioning—deep thinking and making complex calculations—turn out to be so extremely specialized that only a tiny portion of our brains gets involved.

Reading and writing are both higher on the list, with reading aloud right near the top. (Image streaming, the exercise you learned in Chapter 1, is another example of something that engages both hemispheres fully.)

Yet the number-one thing that seems to get your whole brain switched on and active is solving simple calculations at a high speed. This research suggests that while doing crossword puzzles and Sudoku will absolutely help to keep your brain sharp, harder isn't always better.

Solving a simple puzzle quickly will engage more of your brain than taking all day to solve a difficult one.

(Of course, solving the difficult one might be more satisfying—this is just about what it takes to stay sharp, not what you do for enjoyment and satisfaction!)

What Cab Drivers Know about Getting Smarter

In the year 2000, a study was published at University College London that used brain-imaging technology to see what happens to the brains of London taxi drivers when they take the extensive training course known as the Knowledge. While GPS technology may one day make the Knowledge a thing of the past, for the past 150 years or so it has been the most exhaustive and difficult exam of its kind in the world. Typically, a would-be cabbie will wind up studying for nearly three years and taking the exam as many as a dozen times before demonstrating the level of insight into the streets of London that is required to be licensed by the city as a black cab driver.

In line with what we have been learning about neuroplasticity, the size and shape of London taxi drivers' brains changed dramatically during their years of study. In particular, the part of the brain relating to memory and navigation became notably larger than in a typical person. These differences were most pronounced while drivers were actually engaged in doing the Knowledge and were directly related to the amount of time they spent on it. Once again, the brain's capacity to change and grow in order to meet the demands placed on it was clearly on view.

Other studies have shown similar results among chess champions, jugglers, even video gamers. One study followed a group of teenage girls playing Tetris over a three-month period and discovered that their cortical pathways were both physically stronger and more active than they had been before the study began.

One way to understand the significance of all this research is to think about how much the world changed when the Romans began building roads across Europe and Asia. As trade between countries and different parts of the world became easier and easier, the entire basis for the world economy changed. In the same way, as we build new and more efficient pathways for information to travel upon within the brain, the possibilities for creativity, critical thinking, and inspired action increase exponentially.

The fact that brain training works is no longer in question. What remains to be discovered is how best to make use of the neuroplasticity of the brain to improve performance and how far these changes can go in the delay and ultimately even prevention of dementia and Alzheimer's disease.

In the rest of this chapter, I will share five unconventional strategies for staying sharp at any age that have each been documented as making a discernible and sometimes dramatic difference in mental well-being. Following any one of them will make a noticeable difference to your mental "sharpness," but used in combination your results will soar!

STRATEGY NUMBER ONE: PHYSICAL EXERCISE FOR MENTAL HEALTH

The Ancient Romans had a saying that has become the motto of many modern institutions, including the Royal Army Physical Training Corps:

Mens sana in corpore sano—
A healthy mind in a healthy body

Today, modern brain research has shown us that this is more than just a catchy slogan. Exercise brings blood to your brain, providing glucose for energy and oxygen to reduce toxicity and create an overall healthy environment. Some studies have even indicated that aerobic exercise just twice a week halves your risk of general dementia and cuts your risk of Alzheimer's by as much as 60 percent.

While the positive benefits of physical exercise increase over time, even a small amount of exercise begun today will have a positive impact on your brainpower in both the short and the long term. Yet no matter how much I talk about the benefits of physical exercise, I know that isn't enough to get you to get more of it. After all, if knowing that getting exercise helps you to build muscle, lose fat, feel great, enhance your mental clarity, and increase your sex drive isn't going to do it, knowing that it cuts the odds of losing your faculties when you get older probably won't do it either.

The problem isn't that you don't know what to do—it's that you haven't yet linked pleasure to the thought of exercise. As I guide you through this next technique, we are going to make the idea of moving your body much more appealing, using the superstate of motivation you have already created and linking it to getting exercise. As always, read through all the steps before putting the technique into action . . .

MOTIVATION POWER

Read the technique all the way through before you start.

1. Rate on a scale of 1 to 10 how strong your motivation to exercise is. 1 is the weakest, 10 the strongest.

2. Think of something you are already motivated to do. It may be something you feel particularly passionate about, like your favorite hobby or pastime, a political cause, being with a loved one, or spending time with your family.

3. If nothing springs to mind immediately ask yourself: if you had won a lottery jackpot—how motivated would you be to go and collect the check? Or how motivated would you be to save the life of your closest friend? Or if the most attractive person in the world asked you out on a date—how motivated would you be to say yes?

4. Whatever motivates you most right now, I'd like you to visualize the scene—seeing it through your own eyes as though it's here now. See again what you would see, hear what you would hear, and feel exactly how being motivated feels.

5. Now notice all the details of the scene. Make the colors richer, bolder, and brighter. Make the sounds clearer and the feelings stronger. As the feelings build to a peak, squeeze together your finger and thumb.

Continued

6. Keep going through that motivational movie. As soon as it finishes, start it again, all the time feeling that motivation and squeezing your thumb and finger together. See what you saw, hear what you heard, and feel that motivation.

7. STOP! Relax your fingers. Move about a bit before continuing.

8. Are you ready to test your motivation trigger? Squeeze your thumb and finger together and relive that good feeling now. It's important to realize it may not feel as intense, but you can increase your feelings of motivation every time you do this exercise. Now it's time to make the association between feeling motivated and moving your body . . .

9. Squeeze your thumb and finger together and remember what it's like to feel motivated. Now imagine yourself moving your body easily and effortlessly throughout the day. Imagine things going perfectly, going exactly the way you want them to go, finding more and more opportunities to enjoy moving your body in enjoyable ways. See what you'll see, hear what you'll hear, and feel how good it feels. As soon as you have done that, go through it again, still squeezing together your finger and thumb, permanently associating motivation to exercise.

10. Finally, on a scale of 1 to 10, how motivated do you feel to move your body? The higher the number, the easier you will find it to incorporate physical exercise into your daily routine. The lower the number, the more you need to practice the preceding technique.

STRATEGY NUMBER TWO: WHERE DO BRAINS GO TO WORK OUT?

Years ago, my friend Michael Neill introduced me to a series of exercises from a field called educational kinesiology. These exercises are selected from a larger series of activities known as the "Brain Gym," created by Dr. Paul and Gail Dennison. Each of the exercises is designed to engage your body in the process of switching your whole brain "on" by activating the connections between the left and right hemispheres. In addition, each one is particularly useful in activating the bits of the brain most involved in various learning activities.

While these exercises are extremely simple, they also really work, and they became a regular part of our NLP trainings for many years. You can do them on their own or in any combination. Use them any time during the day when you need a mind break or a boost of mental energy!

The Gravity Glider (helps with logical, sequential thinking)

Cross your ankles, keeping your knees loose. Bend over and let your arms take you down towards the floor. Be sure to breathe while you're down there! When you're ready, uncurl slowly, stacking each vertebra on top of the one beneath, bringing your head and neck up slowly and last. Repeat up to three times, then change the cross of your ankles and do it again.

Cross Crawl (helps with reading, clear speaking, and athletic performance)

Move one arm and the opposite leg at the same time, then reverse and repeat for at least a minute. Be sure to cross the midline of the body (from the top of your head down to your feet) as often as possible. If you notice yourself moving the arm and leg from the same side (i.e., right arm/right leg or left arm/left leg), it means your brain is temporarily switched off. Doing this exercise will switch it back on and leave it in the "on" position for hours to come!

The Elephant (helps with math and spelling)

Bend your knees, bringing your head to your left shoulder, and point across the room with your left arm. Draw a "lazy eight" with your whole arm, coming up in the middle from left to right and then from right to left. Trace out past the ends of your finger-tips with your eyes. Then repeat with your right arm. Aim for at least 30 seconds per side.

Thymus Tapping (helps with overall levels of energy and well-being)

Place your feet shoulder width apart. Count down two to three ribs from the notch at the top of your rib cage and begin a gentle tapping rhythm with your fingers or a loose fist in the center of your chest. For extra energy, lift your eyes up about 45 degrees above the horizon and breathe deeply while you tap. This exercise will serve to both energize and relax you. It has also been found to strengthen your thymus gland, which is responsible for the immune function in the body.

STRATEGY NUMBER THREE: YOUR PORTABLE MEMORY BANK

I remember going to dinner once with Dr. Win Wenger, author of over 50 books on creativity, accelerated learning, and brain/mind development. As we were talking, he began rooting through his pockets as though he had lost something. When I asked him what he was looking for, he said, "My portable memory bank."

He then explained that the unifying trait he had found in all the geniuses he had studied was that they had learned to value their own ideas, not just by affirming that value but by recording the ideas in writing. He called the technique of jotting down your insights and creative ideas into a notebook a "portable memory bank," and cited great minds throughout history like Leonardo da Vinci, Michael Faraday, and Albert Einstein among those whose active use of notebooks both unleashed and reinforced their genius.

People say they won't write down their ideas because they don't have anything worth recording, but I say they don't have anything worth recording because they won't write down their ideas.

CALL TO ACTION

Write it down

Sometimes the most powerful techniques are also the simplest. If you want to unleash your genius, go out and get a notebook and pen and carry them around with you at all times. Whenever you have an idea, jot it down. You may be surprised by what you discover!

STRATEGY NUMBER FOUR: CONTROL STRESS

Most people are aware of the negative impact of stress on our physical health. But a lesser-known effect of the stress hormone cortisol is that it can damage the cells of the hippocampus, the part of your brain responsible for both learning and memory. Chronic or intense stress can actually lead the part of the brain that protects it from stress to switch itself off, allowing the memory circuits of the brain to be overwhelmed and flooded with cortisol. This is one of the theories as to why traumatic experiences are often accompanied by full or partial amnesia—the bit of the brain responsible for remembering temporarily or permanently ceases to function.

Fortunately, our bodies have a built-in "fail-safe" mechanism for overriding an overzealous stress response and returning our systems to a state of natural calm. It's located in your physical heart, and neurocardiologists call it your "heart brain." This heart brain has at least 40,000 neurons—as many as are found in some subsections of the brain. In fact, it has such elaborate neurological circuitry that it is capable of learning, remembering, feeling, and sensing things independently of the brain in the head.

Every time your heart beats, it is sending information to your head brain, which influences perceptions, emotions, and awareness, as well as having a regulatory influence on many of the nervous system signals—including the stress response.

What this means is that the human heart is not just a pump for blood, it is the physical control center that determines whether to trigger the sympathetic or parasympathetic nervous system—the stress response or natural relaxation.

The technique I'm about to share with you was created by the Institute of Heartmath, a nonprofit-research center that has spent the past 20 years studying the role of the physical heart in health, intelligence, and well-being. You can use it any time you are experiencing a stressful feeling in your body or an overly busy mind. It will help you to feel better almost immediately—usually in less than a minute. In addition, it will assist you in bringing your brain back on line so that you can be at your best when you need it the most . . .

FREEZE FRAME

Read the technique all the way through before you start.

1. Notice what kinds of thoughts you are thinking. If you like, write them down.

2. Take a quick time-out, like "freezing the frame" on a film or video clip. Take three slow and gentle breaths into the area of your physical heart, deliberately shifting your attention out of your head and onto the area around your heart.

3. Next, think a happy thought—it can be a memory of a positive experience or a thought about someone or something that makes you smile. Make sure to associate into the experience or thought until you are feeling a positive feeling in your body.

4. While feeling a positive feeling, ask your heart, "What would be a more efficient response to my situation, one that would minimize my stress, now and in the future?"

5. Listen to your answer. If there is any action to be taken, take it as soon as you can. If not, simply enjoy the good feeling in your body and "unfreeze" your life!

It's okay if you don't "hear" an answer to your question. You may simply feel calmer, or get a sudden insight into the situation or intuition about how best to handle the situation. Whatever happens is the wisdom of your "heart-brain" in action.

STRATEGY NUMBER FIVE: SLEEP WELL TO THINK WELL

In his excellent book *Brain Rules*, brain researcher Dr. John Medina shares research into sleep deprivation that shows that after a certain amount of time without sleep, people experience negative effects ranging from mood swings and nausea to symptoms of forgetfulness and paranoia similar to those associated with Alzheimer's disease.

On the flip side, there is also ample research to show that a good night's sleep (or at the very least, a well-timed power nap) can help consolidate learning and trigger insights and creative breakthroughs.

While I have written an entire book on how to create healthier sleep patterns for yourself, the following technique will serve as a "quick fix" you can use any time you need to refresh your body and mind.

THE POWER NAP

Read the technique all the way through before you start.

1. Begin by moving your attention down to your feet. Notice the feelings of your feet, their relative warmth or coolness, and their weight.

2. Take a deep breath in, then let it out, and as you do so imagine a pleasant, warm, and relaxing feeling developing in your feet.

3. Now take another deep, gentle breath in and imagine that warm and relaxing feeling traveling up the legs to your knees. Say the number "one" in your mind.

4. Allow that warm and relaxing feeling to penetrate your muscles and bones, gently spreading and soothing as it moves.

5. When you are ready, take another gentle deep breath and imagine that warm relaxing feeling rising up to your waist, and as it does say "two."

6. Breathing in, pull the feeling of ease and relaxation up to your shoulders, and say "three."

7. Let the relaxation move along your shoulders and all the way down your arms to your hands.

8. Breathing in, let the feeling go all the way up, right to the top of your head. Say "four" and spread those good, relaxing feelings all over your body.

9. Now, say in your mind the number "five" and imagine that relaxing feeling doubling, as if a new, fresh flow of relaxation was descending from above your head and joining the warm relaxing feelings already going on inside you.

10. And as you imagine this flow of relaxation spreading back down your body, imagine any and all tension being washed down along with it, draining out of your body through the bottoms of your feet, making room for you to be refilled on each breath with new, relaxing, refreshing energy. Make sure you take a few moments to really enjoy those feelings of relaxation.

11. Pause for a little while to notice the feeling and then, if you wish, repeat the sequence. The more you practice the technique, the more effective it becomes.

Stay with this feeling as long as you wish. If at this point your attention wanders or you would like to close your eyes, that's perfectly okay—you will arise refreshed and alert in just a few minutes . . .

THE WHOLE CHAPTER IN ONE PAGE

- When it comes to your brain, the rule of thumb is the same as when it comes to the musculature of your body—use it or lose it!

- The brain will adapt and change in response to specific challenges, in the same way as the muscles in the body will develop and strengthen in response to the physical demands of exercise and athletic challenges. This ability is called "neuroplasticity."

- The number-one way to get your whole brain switched on and active is solving simple calculations at a high speed.

- Physical exercise is a key to optimal brain functioning.

- Certain patterns of movement balance left and right brain functioning, ensuring that your brain is "switched on."

- Stress is the number-one enemy of learning.

- When you sleep better, you think better.

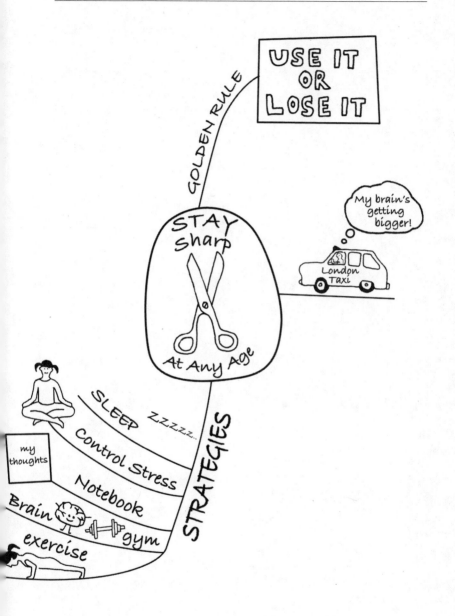

SOME FINAL THOUGHTS ON GETTING SMARTER

As we reach the end of our time together, you have probably already begun to experience yourself as smarter. You may have noticed things changing for the better in your ability to learn, understand, and interact with the world around you. But however much you have already seen, rest assured that the real excitement is yet to come.

After more than 20 years in the field of human potential, I feel like I've barely begun to scratch the surface of what's possible. The human mind is amazing!

As you take your own extraordinary mind and brain out into the world, you have the potential to see things that have never been seen before and to discover what has not yet been discovered. You are unique. Nobody can do things exactly the way that you do, and as you share more of your unique gifts with the world, the world itself will become a richer place.

One thing that will certainly make this a better planet is if we all get at least a little bit smarter. And whatever problems we may have created in the world as a species, the capacity to solve those problems is alive within us even now.

Writing this book has been an extraordinary journey for me, as I've had to face up to some of the limitations from my past even as I opened up to new, exciting possibilities for the future. I thank you for investing your time and energy into making yourself smarter, and I wish you every success in life. May you use your extraordinary capacity and unique genius to create a better world for all of us!

To your success!

Paul McKenna
Los Angeles 2011

SMARTER TECHNIQUES

THANKS TO

Dr. Ronald Ruden, Dr. Richard Bandler, Mari Roberts, Gillian Blease, Julia Lloyd, Kate Davey, Doug Young, Alex Tuppen, Dr. Natheera Indrasanen, Steve Shaw, Mike Osborne, Michael Breen, Steve Crabb

We hope you enjoyed this Hay House book. If you'd like to receive our
online catalog featuring additional information on Hay House books
and products, or if you'd like to find out more about the
Hay Foundation, please contact:

Hay House, Inc., P.O. Box 5100, Carlsbad, CA 92018-5100
(760) 431-7695 or (800) 654-5126
(760) 431-6948 (fax) or (800) 650-5115 (fax)
www.hayhouse.com® • www.hayfoundation.org

• • •

Published and distributed in Australia by:
Hay House Australia Pty. Ltd., 18/36 Ralph St., Alexandria NSW 2015
Phone: 612-9669-4299 • *Fax:* 612-9669-4144 • www.hayhouse.com.au

Published and distributed in the United Kingdom by:
Hay House UK, Ltd., Astley House, 33 Notting Hill Gate,
London W11 3JQ • *Phone:* 44-20-3675-2450 • *Fax:* 44-20-3675-2451
www.hayhouse.co.uk

Published and distributed in the Republic of South Africa by:
Hay House SA (Pty), Ltd., P.O. Box 990, Witkoppen 2068
info@hayhouse.co.za • www.hayhouse.co.za

Published in India by: Hay House Publishers India,
Muskaan Complex, Plot No. 3, B-2, Vasant Kunj, New Delhi 110 070
Phone: 91-11-4176-1620 • *Fax:* 91-11-4176-1630 • www.hayhouse.co.in

Distributed in Canada by:
Raincoast Books, 2440 Viking Way, Richmond, B.C. V6V 1N2
Phone: 1-800-663-5714 • *Fax:* 1-800-565-3770 • www.raincoast.com

• • •

Take Your Soul on a Vacation

Visit www.HealYourLife.com® to regroup, recharge, and reconnect with
your own magnificence. Featuring blogs, mind-body-spirit news, and
life-changing wisdom from Louise Hay and friends.

Visit www.HealYourLife.com today!

Paul McKenna, Ph.D., is described by Ryan Seacrest as "a cross between the Dr. Phil and Tony Robbins of Britain." Recently named by the *London Times* as one of the world's leading and most important modern gurus, alongside Nelson Mandela and the Dalai Lama, he is Britain's best-selling nonfiction author, selling 8,000 books a week in 35 countries— a total of 8 million books in the last decade. He has worked his unique brand of personal transformation with Hollywood movie stars, Olympic gold medalists, rock stars, leading business achievers, and royalty. Over the past 20 years, Paul McKenna has helped millions of people successfully quit smoking, lose weight, overcome insomnia, eliminate stress, and increase self-confidence. Dr. McKenna has appeared on *The Dr. Oz Show, Good Morning America, The Ellen DeGeneres Show, Rachael Ray, Anderson Live,* and *The Early Show.* He is regularly watched on TV by hundreds of millions of people in 42 countries around the world.

Dr. McKenna has consistently astounded his audiences and clients by proving how small changes in people's lives can yield huge results, whether it's curing someone of a lifelong phobia or clearing up deep-seated issues in a matter of minutes. He currently hosts his own TV show on Hulu, where he interviews the most interesting people in the world. His guests include Simon Cowell, Harvey Weinstein, Rachael Ray, Sir Roger Moore, Roger Daltrey, Tony Robbins, Paul Oakenfold, and Sir Ken Robinson. Website: www.mckenna.com